Corrections and Post-Traumatic Stress Symptoms

Daniel S. Murphy
Appalachian State University

CAROLINA ACADEMIC PRESS
Durham, North Carolina

Copyright © 2012
Daniel S. Murphy
All Rights Reserved

Library of Congress Cataloging-in-Publication Data

Murphy, Daniel S.
  Corrections and post-traumatic stress symptoms / Daniel S. Murphy.
     p. cm.
  Includes index.
  ISBN 978-1-61163-192-0 (alk. paper)
  1. Prisoners--Mental health. 2. Prisoners--Mental health services. 3. Post-traumatic stress disorder. I. Title.

  RC451.4.P68M87 2012
  616.85'21--dc23   2012013523

Carolina Academic Press
700 Kent Street
Durham, NC 27701
Telephone (919) 489-7486
Fax (919) 493-5668
www.cap-press.com

Printed in the United States of America

Layout and cover design by Mark H. Suggs, *abi*GRAPHICS.com

Acknowledgments

I share my loving appreciation for my Mom and Dad who gave me life and saved my life. A special thanks to Mr. Gene E. Lynn for providing constant support throughout my time of need and continuing forth.

Summary

Those sentenced to prison bring with them individual characteristics acquired prior to incarceration. This study assesses the effect of pre-prison experiences on adjustment to the prison environment. Regression analysis indicates that pre-prison experiences are significantly related to the likelihood of participating in, or being exposed to, elements of the incarceration experience that may cause Post-Traumatic Stress Symptoms (PTSS). A second component of this study assesses the relationship between elements of the incarceration experience and PTSS. Regression analysis indicates that aspects of the incarceration experience constitute traumatic stressors that cause PTSS in some individuals. This study also assesses the relationship between pre-prison experiences and PTSS, independent of the incarceration experience, as well as assessing the relationship between a combination of the pre-prison and in-prison independent variables with development of PTSS. Data for this study are drawn from surveys administered to 208 men released from prison in a Midwestern state.

Contents

Chapter 1. Prison and Post-Traumatic Stress Symptoms
    Introduction...1
    Post-Traumatic Stress 3
    Theory 3
    Research Questions 4
    Pre-Incarceration 5
    Incarceration...7
        Post-Traumatic Stress Symptoms......................7
        The Pains of Imprisonment 8
    Post-Incarceration....................................10
        Stigma and Blocked Opportunity.....................11

Chapter 2. Literature Review
    The Sociological Foundation of Criminal
    Justice Research 15
    The Prison Population................................19
    Post-Traumatic Stress Disorder 22
    Pre-Incarceration 26
        Streetwise and Criminality 26
        Preparation for Prison 28
        Family and Negative Parenting..................... 29

    Incarceration 30
        Psychological Consequences 30
        The Mentally Ill Offender........................... 32
        PTSS as Precursor 34
        Environmental Factors............................. 35
        The Inmate Economy 35
        The Convict Code 37
        Learned Helplessness 39
    Victimization.. 40
        The General Population 40
        The Prison Experience 41
        Prison Domain–Specific Lifestyle Theory 43
    Hypotheses... 45
        Hypothesis 1...................................... 46
        Hypothesis 2...................................... 48
        Hypothesis 3...................................... 48
        Hypothesis 4: Fully Recursive Model 49

Chapter 3. Methodology
    Research Approach................................... 51
    Population Sample.................................... 52
    Data Collection Procedures 53
    Researcher-Respondent Interaction:
    Convict Criminology.................................. 53
    Verification Questions 55
    Measures.. 56
        Control Variables 56
    Variable Construction 57
        Streetwise.. 57

Pre-Prison Criminality	57
Frequency in the System	58
Negative Parenting	58
Participation in the Inmate Economy	59
Victimization	60
Witness Victimization	61
Convict Code	61
Post-Traumatic Stress Symptoms	62
Post-Traumatic Stress: Symptoms vs. Diagnostic Criteria	62

Chapter 4. Analysis

Zero-Order Correlation	65
Multicollinearity	66
Hypotheses	68
Regression Analysis	69
Hypothesis 1: Findings	71
Model 1: Effects of Pre-Prison Variables on Inmate Economy (Adj. R^2 = .34)	71
Model 2: Effects of Pre-Prison Variables on In-Prison Victimization (Adj. R^2 = .15)	73
Model 3: Effects of Pre-Prison Variables on Witnessing Victimization in Prison (Adj. R^2 = .36)	74
Model 4: Effects of Pre-Prison Variables on Adherence to the Convict Code (Adj. R^2 = .31)	76
Hypothesis 2: Findings	79
Model 5: Effects of In-Prison Variables on Development of PTSS (Adj. R^2 = .22)	79

  Hypothesis 3: Findings 81
    Model 6: Effects of Pre-Prison Variables on Developing PTSS Independent of the Prison Experience (Adj. R^2 = .22) 81
    Analysis of the Relationship Between a Combined Set of Pre-Prison and In-Prison Independent Variables With Development of PTSS 83
    Model 7: Effect of Combined Set of Pre-Prison and In-Prison Independent Variables on Developing PTSS Independent of the Prison Experience (Adj. R^2 = .33) 85

Chapter 5. Summary, Discussion, Conclusion
  Research Objective 87
  Summary of Findings 88
    Pre-Prison Variables on Prison Adjustment: Direct and/or Indirect Effects 88
    In-Prison Variables on PTSS: Direct and/or Indirect Effects 91
    Pre-Prison Variables on PTSS: Direct and/or Indirect Effects 93
    Combined Pre-Prison and In-Prison Independent Variables on Development of PTSS: Direct and/or Indirect Effects 94
  Elements of the Hypotheses Not Supported 95
  Limitations 97
  Implications 97
  Recommendations for Future Research 99
  Social and Economic Costs of Incarceration 102
    Post-Incarceration: An "Army" of Releasees 102
    Incarceration: Costs to the Tax Payer 104

Appendix 1. Independent Variables for Hypothesis 1 107

Appendix 2. Operational Definitions of In-Prison Dependent Variables 113

Appendix 3. Post-Traumatic Stress Diagnostic Scale: UM-CIDI Dependent Variable 119

Appendix 4. Operational Definitions of Pre-Prison Control Variables 122

References 125

Index 135

Chapter 1. Prison and Post-Traumatic Stress Symptoms

Introduction

It is reasonable to posit that pre-prison experiences affect adjustment to the prison environment (Sykes, 1958), and that in-prison experiences affect the offender's adjustment upon release (Murphy, 2003). "Thus, an inmate's ability to deal with incarceration is contingent on the history of experiences that [an] inmate brings to prison and hold significance for how successful the inmate will be in facing impending extramural challenges" upon release (Adams, 1992, p. 278).

This book explores the relationship between pre-prison experiences and adjustment to prison. It also examines the relationship between prison experiences and post-traumatic stress symptoms (PTSS). In addition, the study examines the relationship between pre-prison experiences and PTSS independent of the incarceration experience, as well as the relationship between a combination of the pre-prison and in-prison independent variables with PTSS. The analyses of the research data may provide a foundation for a discussion of the societal challenges posed by the enormous numbers of people returning to the community after incarceration.

Figure 1 depicts the elements analyzed in the present study. The path of model 1 analyzes the effect of each of the pre-prison variables on increasing the likelihood of each of the in-prison variables. The path of model 2 analyzes the effect of each of the in-prison variables on increasing the likelihood of developing PTSS. The path of model 3 analyzes the effect of each of the pre-prison variables on increasing the likelihood of PTSS independent of the prison experience. The path of the fully recursive model 4 analyzes the effect of each of the pre-prison and in-prison variables on increasing the likelihood of PTSS.

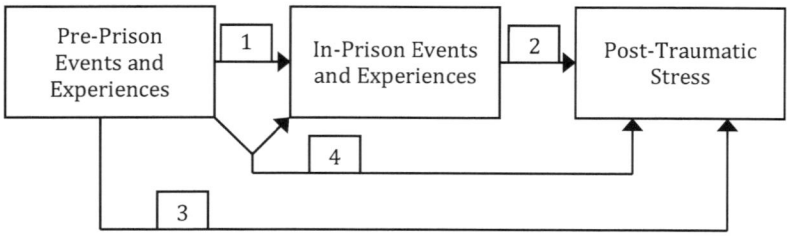

Figure 1. Pre-Prison, In-Prison, and Post Traumatic Stress

Post-Traumatic Stress

Post-traumatic stress symptoms (PTSS) are predicated upon an external catastrophic traumatic event, rather than an individual internal condition. PTSS was first delineated in the Diagnostic Statistical Manual of Mental Disorders (DSM; 1980) as a traumatic event conceptualized as a catastrophic stressor that is outside the range of usual human experience. This study included an exploration of the relationships between in-prison traumatic events and the development of PTSS, as well as the onset of PTSS independent of the incarceration experience. The clinical definition of PTSS has been expanded and clarified in the 4th edition of the Diagnostic Statistical Manual (DSM-IV-TR; 2000).

Theory

This study bridges the importation model (Irwin & Cressey, 1962) and the deprivation model (Sykes, 1958), which are theoretical lenses through which to view the origins of the convict code and adjustment to the prison environment. Proponents of the deprivation model stress the importance of the prison social environment in forming inmate attitudes and self-perceptions. Conversely, those who support the importation model stress the importance of values that inmates bring to the prison experience, values learned in the free world (often the code of the streets) and/or in their criminal life. Supporters of the integrated model (Thomas, 1970) advocate combining elements of the deprivation and importation models to explain inmate adjustment patterns.

The theoretical perspective that guides the investigation of the relationship between aspects of the prison experience and PTSS is a place-specific application of lifestyle theory (Wooldredge, 1994, 1998, 1999; Wooldredge & Carboneau, 1998). Prison-specific lifestyle theory builds upon opportunity theories, most notably routine activities theory (Cohen & Felson, 1979) and lifestyle/exposure theory (Hindelang, Gottfredson, & Garofalo, 1978).

Application of domain-specific lifestyle theory offers one explanation for the variation in victimization within the prison environment. The relationship between in-prison victimization and witnessing victimization as potential causal mechanisms in the development of PTSS was investigated along with how participation in the inmate economy and adherence to the convict code serve as mechanisms that may lead to the development of PTSS. Further, elements of pre-prison experiences and in-prison experiences that rise to the level of traumatic stressor that may result in PTSS (Goff, Rose, Rose & Purves, 2007) were examined.

Research Questions

The research questions explored in this study include: (a) Do pre-prison variables, including, streetwise, pre-prison criminality, frequency in the system, race, education, age first incarcerated (Appendix 1) affect adjustment to the prison environment? (b) Do aspects of the incarceration experience, including participation in the inmate economy, victimization, witnessing victimization, and adherence to the convict code (Appendix 2) contribute to the development of PTSS for some prisoners? (c) Do pre-prison variables affect onset of PTSS (Appendix 3) independent of the prison experience? and (d) Is there a relationship between pre-prison events and experiences, in-prison events and experiences with onset of PTSS? This preliminary study tests relationships among pre-prison, in-prison, and post-prison variables by analyzing data collected from 208 men released from state penitentiaries in a Midwestern state.

Analysis of the process of moving from pre-prison to in-prison to post-prison environments may provide information that guides the development of programs designed to better assist individuals adjust to incarceration, as well as programs designed to assist individuals adjust to post-incarceration life. Specifically, the findings may foster understanding of conditions in the prison environment that cause PTSS. Further, findings may guide development of programs designed to assist prisoners who enter prison with PTSS, as well as those who develop symptoms while incarcerated. These findings may also provide information that will guide development of social programs designed to increase safety and security for the citizenry while providing needed support for the released prisoner.

Pre-Incarceration

Prior to incarceration, prisoners disproportionately experience economic and social disadvantage where violence, substance abuse, family disruption, and traumatic experiences are common (Hochstetler, Murphy, & Simons, 2004). Demographic variables such as race, education, and age first incarcerated, as well as factors occurring in youth, such as frequency of out-of-home placement, reintegration services, poverty, physical abuse, sexual abuse, and witnessing violence have been linked to adult imprisonment (Ryan, Davis, & Yang, 2001; Greene, Haney, & Hurtado, 2000). Additionally, lack of self-control has been linked to involvement in illegal and analogous behaviors that result in incarceration (Gottfredson & Hirschi, 1990). People who have low levels of self-control are more likely to engage in criminal behavior and are thus more likely to experience incarceration. Therefore, the importation model suggests that prisoners import norms and values acquired prior to incarceration into the prison environment, and that these norms and values affect adjustment to prison as well as influence the subculture of the convict code.

Pre-prison experiences affect how individuals adjust to the prison environment (importation model). Adams (1992), in a review of empirical research, reports that demographic characteristics such as age, race, sex, marital status (Jaman, 1972; Myers & Levy, 1978; Toch & Adams, 1989), drug use, emotional disorder, mental retardation (Toch & Adams), criminal history (Toch & Adams), prior incarceration experiences, employment history, and educational achievement (Zamble & Porporino, 1988; Wright, 1991) affected prison adjustment.

In addition to the effect pre-prison experiences have on individuals, the resultant attitudes and patterns of action that individuals develop as a result of those experiences have a direct effect on the interactive processes of the prison population at large. For example, if an individual has violent tendencies prior to incarceration, this individual is likely to import violence into the prison setting, thereby raising the likelihood of the victimization of others.

Knowing which individuals entering prison are likely to be aggressors and which will likely be victims may inform prison policy and guide development of programs designed to minimize prison violence. At the individual level, programs designed to help the inmate adjust to the prison environment may reduce potential traumatic stressors such as personal victimization and witnessing the victimization of others, thereby reducing the likelihood of the onset of PTSS caused by the incarceration experience (Goff et al., 2007). At the institutional level, such programs may foster a greater sense of security and as such may reduce the traumatic stressor fear of victimization, thereby reducing the likelihood of PTSS as result of the incarceration experience.

Incarceration

Post-Traumatic Stress Symptoms

The constellation of symptoms associated with post-traumatic stress develops after an individual has suffered a catastrophic traumatic event. These symptoms compose a syndrome that is ongoing and requires specific treatment. Studies have shown that some inmates do not cope well with imprisonment and that traumatic events encountered in prison may result in maladaptive responses including emotional disorders (Adams, 1992; Bonta & Gendreau, 1990; Guthrie, 1999; Gendreau

& Keyes, 2001). In support of this study, Brinded and colleagues found the prevalence rate of individuals suffering PTSS in prison to be higher than in the general population (Brinded et al., 2001; Goff et al., 2007).

The individual exposed to catastrophic trauma may develop a hyper-reactive response to a variety of stimuli that may result in multiple types of negative behaviors. The hyper-reactive response may be triggered by environmental cues reminiscent of the catastrophic trauma of origin. Given the negative events and experiences endemic in the prison setting, it may be that the very nature of the prison environment produces and perpetuates PTSS. Therefore, recognizing PTSS as a health problem in prison populations is critical.

Understanding the relationship between experiences of prison and the development of PTSS may lay a foundation for the development of prison policy to correct conditions in the prison environment that lead to PTSS. In addition, exploration of the relationship between prison conditions and the development of PTSS may assist in developing programs to both address the needs of individual prisoners suffering PTSS within the prison setting and assist those who "export" (Murphy, 2003) PTSS acquired in prison to the community.

The Pains of Imprisonment

The typology developed by Sykes (1958) provides insight into aspects of incarceration that may lead to the development of PTSS. In *The Society of Captives: A Study of a Maximum Security Prison*, Sykes devotes a chapter, "The Pains of Imprisonment," to what he considers 5 major losses—or "deprivations"—a prisoner must endure. The first deprivation addressed is loss of liberty. In addition to physical and geographic restrictions, prisoners often experience the pain of isolation from family and community. Isolation may lead to increased levels of stress (Gendreau & Keyes, 2001), which in turn may rise to the level of a traumatic stressor that results in PTSS.

The second great loss described by Sykes (1958) is the deprivation of goods and services. The prisoner cannot acquire any personal luxuries that might bring him physical or emotional comfort: only the base requirements of human survival are provided within the strictures of prison. Such deprivation may add to the ongoing stressors associated with the prison experience and may result in PTSS.

Third, prisoners face the deprivation of heterosexual relationships (Sykes, 1958). In prison, normal avenues of sexual release are forbidden. Prisoners who are otherwise heterosexual may engage in homosexual activity to meet their sexual needs which may result in rape (Prison Rape Elimination Act, 2003). Research has shown the catastrophic experience of rape to be a causal mechanism in the development of PTSS (Kizer, 1996).

The fourth great loss Sykes (1958) describes is deprivation of autonomy. Prisoners are not allowed to make the simple decisions of life taken for granted by most, such as choosing when to get up in the morning or when to go to bed at night, or choosing what to wear, what to eat, or what to drink. The loss of autonomy may result in learned helplessness and despair that may lead to PTSS.

The last deprivation Sykes (1958) describes is the loss of security. In the prison environment the potential exists for victimization at any moment. Subject to such a volatile environment, prisoners are forced to protect themselves against real or imagined threats by fellow prisoners and prison guards. The total institution of prison confines the victim with the victimizer (Goffman, 1961, 1963). Relentless fear of victimization and the trauma that results from being victimized have been shown to cause PTSS.

Post-Incarceration

Some prisoners who have endured the vicissitudes of the incarceration experience will develop PTSS. Former prisoners who have developed PTSS, or ancillary psychological symptoms as consequence of the prison experience, may pose serious risks for society in that they may export conditions acquired during the prison experience back to the community to which they return (Murphy, 2003).

Identifying and providing assistance for individuals in prison who suffer from PTSS or exhibit the potential for these symptoms may be cost-effective. Such assistance may reduce the likelihood of antisocial behavior after the prisoner's release, thereby increasing the safety and security of the citizenry. The alternative is to release prisoners suffering with PTSS directly into the community, potentially igniting an array of costly problems for individuals and society.

Incarceration is socially and psychologically debilitating (Schmid & Jones, 1993; Haney & Zimbardo, 1998). Negative aspects of the prison experience may result in psychological damage including PTSS. Given the sheer magnitude of the number of prisoners returning to the community each year, the implications for society are enormous. In 2008, 735,454 individuals were released from the adverse conditions of prison (Bureau of Justice Statistics Bulletin, 2009). The present study explores the possibility that certain prisoners develop PTSS as result of the prison experience and therefore pose unique challenges for society upon their release.

Some researchers contend that incarceration itself is a predictor of post-incarceration recidivism (Petersilia, 1995). Further, the symptoms associated with post-traumatic stress may increase the likelihood of recidivism. Programs designed to reintegrate ex-offenders suffering PTSS as productive members of society are required to reduce recidivism, to reduce the number of individuals in prison, and ultimately ease the financial burden of incarceration incurred by the taxpayer.

Stigma and Blocked Opportunity

Prisoners suffering PTSS may pose unique concerns for society. There is a critical need for programs designed to help individuals suffering PTSS acquired in prison adjust through the post-incarceration process.

Newly released prisoners face a number of challenges and obstacles. PTSS developed in prison (Goff et al., 2007) or independent of the prison experience may exacerbate the difficulties associated with reintegration. Some of the challenges faced include loss of connection to family, segregation, stigmatization, lack of mobility, lack of job opportunities, and wage inequality (O'Brien, 2001). Specific elements of the prison experience may lead to the development of PTSS. The need for prerelease programs designed to assist these individuals in the reintegration process is great.

Some prisoners may lack schooling and/or employment experience prior to incarceration. Others possess talents that enhance employability, yet incarceration erodes these skills. Further, decades of incarceration can place them technologically behind in their trade. Those who are fortunate enough to obtain post-incarceration employment face wage inequality and limited financial growth opportunity (Western, 2002). These challenges are further amplified for those suffering PTSS.

An element of O'Brien's research (2001) indicates that minimizing the socially and psychologically damaging outcomes of incarceration can lead to a reduction in post-incarceration recidivism. This is particularly salient for those who suffer PTSS. In her study, O'Brien concludes that punitive retribution, the focus of contemporary incarceration, diminishes self-esteem. Low levels of self-esteem may hinder efforts to obtain legitimate opportunities towards social reintegration, leading to the pursuit of illegitimate opportunities that increase the likelihood of crime and recidivism. Ex-prisoners who suffer PTSS may experience more difficulty in finding gainful employment compared to those released from prison who do not develop PTSS. Thus, the likelihood of recidivism for those suffering PTSS may be higher than for those who do not develop related symptoms.

It is possible that the prison experience itself may lead to PTSS (Goff et al., 2007), and that development of symptoms in turn may increase problems in gaining post-prison employment. Therefore, results of this study may provide information to guide the development of prison programs designed to assist those suffering PTSS in gaining employment upon release.

Analysis of pre-prison variables as they relate to in-prison adjustment may inform policy at the prison level. Prison programs that recognize and incorporate the influences of pre-prison experiences as they affect adjustment to the prison environment may lead to a reduction in the high levels of anxiety experienced by those incarcerated and thereby may reduce the onset of PTSS. Reduction in catastrophic traumas present in the prison setting may in turn lead to a reduction in the development of PTSS.

This analysis also explores the relationship between onset of PTSS and pre-prison experiences, independent of the prison experience. Research has shown PTSS to be a serious problem within the general population (Kessler et al., 1999). The exploration of the relationship between pre-prison experiences and onset of PTSS independent of the incarceration experience may provide information relevant to implementation of social programs designed to assist individuals suffering PTSS. Further, it is important to recognize those entering prison who are experiencing PTSS, for the prison environment may trigger recollections that result in PTS-induced outbursts or violence.

Chapter 2. Literature Review

The Sociological Foundation of Criminal Justice Research

Prison is a social system that affects the social relations of those confined. Prison is a community with distinctive norms, values, and folkways (Clemmer, 1940). Sykes (1958) describes the prison culture as "the society of captives." Just as the context of a neighborhood, community, or society shapes interactions, so too does the structure of prison influence the social processes of those confined.

In the early 19th century the rationale for the first penitentiary was based upon religious doctrine rather than scientific research. The Quakers first applied the strictures of religious redemption of criminals at the Walnut Street Jail in Philadelphia (Bacon, 1995). This was the first penitentiary and became known as the Pennsylvania System. The Quakers believed that prisoners could be reformed if they were given the opportunity to meditate about their past sins and resolve to live a better life. As part of their contrition, prisoners were separated from each other and confined in solitary isolation. The Quakers believed that isolation would foster meditation that would result in rehabilitation.

Later in the 19th century, the focus moved from the redemption of criminals through religious salvation to scientific attempts to identify common characteristics that could predict criminal propensity. The 19th-century penologists viewed prisoners as evolutionary throwbacks who comprised an antisocial class (Giddons, 1985; Lombrosos and Ferro, 1895). This was the first application of the medical model to crime; however, redemption from criminality remained the primary goal.

In the 20th century rehabilitation replaced redemption as the main goal of imprisonment. The medical model was extended within rehabilitation to include the construct that a cure for the criminal condition, a medical malady, could be developed. This led to trained clinicians being added to correctional staff. The clinicians were thought to be in a position to scientifically classify individual criminals and thereby identify a rehabilitation program that would cure specific criminality.

To accommodate the changing orientation from redemption to rehabilitation, bureaucratic systems replaced the authoritarian style of prison management that was associated with the redemptive model. Sociologists began to examine the changes in the prison environment associated with the philosophical change in prison administration. Scholars became interested in the social relations in prison, in particular, the inmate subculture (e.g., Haynes, 1948).

The first sociological inquiries into the subculture of prison were influenced by the dominant structural–functional paradigm of the early 20th century. Structural–functionalism developed as a result of the seminal work of Durkheim (1895/1982), who emphasized the need for empirical analysis of social facts outside the scope of individual behavior such as social systems, cultural norms, and cultural values. Parsons (1937) expanded upon principles espoused by Durkheim to include different action systems. He examined the distinct systems, and also the intersystemic relationships between them. The focus of both perspectives is the development of and maintenance of an orderly system of social interactions. The structural–functional paradigm viewed socialization as the primary mechanism of systemic maintenance.

A second sociological orientation used to analyze the development and functioning of the inmate subculture and social relations within the prison setting is symbolic interaction (Mead, 1934). Symbolic interaction focuses on the social processes that individuals experience which lead to the development of self. Mead describes a feedback loop through which the actions and behaviors of an individual affect how others respond to the individual and that how others treat the individual affects the actions and behaviors of the individual. Some scholars suggest that this bidirectional feedback loop is a component in the process of prisonization/institutionalization. Theories rooted in symbolic interaction explain how inmates learn the norms of the inmate subculture and how these interactions influence their self-concepts and behaviors.

The developmental process of prison subculture is

captured in Cohen and Felson's (1955/1997) research in the formation of subculture in the general population. Cohen suggests that in response to social disparities the underclass is barred from the opportunity of meeting generalized social goals and therefore reacts against the normative values of society at large. Cohen's work on subculture formation supports an unintended consequence of the prison environment. He suggests that subcultures arise when individuals with similar adjustment problems begin interacting. When similar individuals are grouped together during incarceration the environment for the formation of a prison subculture exists. Further, the development of an inmate subculture in which negative norms and values predominate undermines the correctional goal and inculcates prisoners with the norms and values of the convict code. An additional unintended consequence of prisonization is that released prisoners may export the norms and values of the prison subculture to the community upon release (Murphy, 2003).

In addition to the norms and values of the inmate subculture, the very nature of the prison environment may have deleterious effects upon prisoners. A primary objective for this research was to measure the relationship between elements of the incarceration experience and their effect upon increased likelihood of PTSS. The degree to which prison directly affects individuals is still a matter of debate. Several psychological studies have unsuccessfully attempted to identify detrimental effects of imprisonment (Bonta & Gendreau, 1990; Bukstel & Kilmann, 1980; Haney, 1998; Toch, 1984). Gendreau (2001) conducted a meta-analysis of studies that examined the psychological well-being of inmates in response to prison crowding, health risks, long-term incarceration, solitary confinement, short-term detention, and death row. They found only inconclusive evidence as to the detrimental, psychological effects of incarceration. In a review of 90 experimental, psychological studies, Bukstel and Kilmann (1980) concluded that imprisonment was not harmful to all individuals. However, these studies did not focus on the prison-specific contexts that influence individual prisoner behavior. "Notwithstanding the tendency among researchers to talk about prison as if it were some Weberian ideal type, conditions of confinement can vary dramatically along critical dimensions that render one prison a fundamentally different place in which to live from another" (Haney, 1997). Review of the literature indicates that to date only one multilevel study has examined the influence of prison contexts on individual processes and social relationships inside prison (see Wooldredge, Griffin, and Pratt, 2001). Their findings suggest that psychological damage resultant from the prison experience differs among individuals and by correctional contexts.

The Prison Population

An understanding of the scale of the prison population and related costs to society frames and underscores the importance of the effects of pre-prison experiences upon prison adjustment and between elements of the prison experience that may cause PTSS (Goff et al., 2007). The prison population is growing at an alarming rate and has reached a population density unparalleled in the history of the United States. On July 1, 2010, the number of people imprisoned within the Federal Bureau of prisons reached an all-time high of 211,663 (Federal Bureau of Prisons, 2010). Of this population, 84 percent were first-time, nonviolent offenders. The total number of State and Federal inmates grew from 400,000 in 1982, to over 2,400,000 in 2008. This population growth was accompanied by the opening of over 600 State and 55 Federal correctional facilities (Bureau of Justice Statistics [BJS], 2009). If probation and parole are added to incarceration figures, at the end of 2008, 7.3 million U.S. citizens were in jail, in prison, on probation or parole (BJS, 2009a). Roughly one in 31 United States citizens are presently incarcerated or on probation or parole (BJS, 2009). These figures reflect the fact that the U.S. incarcerates the highest percentage of its citizenry, as well as the highest raw number of individual citizens, among all nations of the world (Kopel, 1994; ; Pew Charitable Trusts, 2007).

The overall incarceration rate of State and Federal prisoners confined in 2008 was 754 per 100,000 U.S. residents. Studies of ethnicity and sentencing rate reveal the Blacks were sentenced at a rate of 3,161 per 100,000; Hispanics at a rate of 1,200 per 100,000; and Whites at a rate of 487 per 100,000 (BJS, 2009a; Sentencing Project, 2010). In 2008, almost 40% of the sentenced prisoners were African American (BJS, 2009a). Assuming recent incarceration rates remain unchanged, an estimated 1 of every 20 Americans can expect to serve time in prison during his or her lifetime. For African American men this figure is 32.2 percent, or more than 1 in 3 African American men can expect to serve time in prison over his life span (BJS, 2009a).

Sentencing data reflects the dramatic 84% increase

in the prison population from the mid-1980s through the beginning of 2001. The Bureau of Justice Statistics attributes the sharp increase in the prison population to "the war on drugs." (BJS, 2001a, 2002, 2003b). The mean sentence length per offense type imposed on federal prisoners underscores this statement. In 2002, the mean sentence length for violent felonies was 63.0 months, whereas the mean sentence length for drug felonies was 75.6 months (BJS, 2001a). McCaffrey (1996) summarized the result of the war on drugs on incarceration when he stated:

> We must have law enforcement authorities address the [drug related] issue(s) because if we do not, prevention, education, and treatment messages will not work very well. But having said that, I also believe that we have created an American Gulag based on the failed interdiction efforts of the war on drugs.

As result of the dramatic increase in incarceration numbers, prison overcrowding is a salient issue, for overcrowding influences how individuals adjust to the prison environment. Further, overcrowding contributes to psychological damage, including PTSS, due to increased violence in overcrowded prisons. At year-end 2008, state prisons were operating between 97-109 percent of rated capacity, and the federal prison system was operating at 135 percent of rated capacity (BJS, 2009a). Given the population density within the confines of prison, strategies to reduce overcrowding are required. Reduction in overcrowding may not only reduce violence, but also the prevalence rate of PTSS that results from the prison experience.

Post-Traumatic Stress Disorder

Given that each year hundreds of thousands of people return to the community after completing their prison sentences, some having developed PTSS as result of the incarceration experience, exploration into the relationship between the prison experience and development of PTSS is a salient issue. Following is a review of the literature related to PTSS.

Yehuda and McFarlane (1995) point out the importance of understanding Post Traumatic Stress Disorder (PTSD). They describe the misunderstanding and marginalization of those suffering PTSS. PTSS offers a concept that assists in the recognition of needs and rights of victims, particularly those who have been misunderstood, ignored, or stigmatized.

Recognizing its impact on individuals, the American Psychiatric Association (APA) first added PTSD to the 3rd edition of the Diagnostic Statistical Manual (DSM-III) classification scheme published in 1980. Following is a discussion of the diagnostic criteria for PTSS as it evolved through DSM-III, DSM-III-R (1987), DSM-IV (1994), and DSM-IV-TR (2000). The significant change ushered in by the PTSD concept was the stipulation that the causal etiological agent was outside the individual, and that a traumatic event—as opposed to an inherent individual weakness—causes PTSD (APA, 1987).

In the DSM-III formulation, a traumatic event was conceptualized as a catastrophic stressor that was outside the range of usual and expected human experience. Traumatic events were considered clearly different from the very painful stressors that constitute the normal vicissitudes of life such as divorce, failure, rejection, serious illness, financial reverses, and so forth.

As delineated in DSM-III, specific criteria exist for the diagnosis of PTSD. The "stressor criterion" specifies that a person had been exposed to a catastrophic event involving actual or threatened death or injury, or a threat to physical integrity (APA, 1994). The "intrusive recollection criterion" includes symptoms that are the most distinctive and readily identifiable symptoms of PTSD. For individuals with PTSD the traumatic event remains, sometimes for decades or a lifetime, a dominating psychological experience that retains its power to evoke panic, terror, dread, grief, or despair, as manifested in daytime fantasies, traumatic nightmares, and psychotic reenactments known as *PTSD flashbacks*.

Traumatic stimuli that trigger recollections of the original event have the power to evoke mental images, emotional responses, metabolic change, and psychological reactions associated with the trauma of origin (APA, 1987). Further, PTSD is associated with increased risk for depression, anxiety, alcohol or substance use disorders, hypertension, bronchial asthma, peptic ulcers, and other diseases (Davidson, 2001). It is important to note that PTSD does not necessarily develop immediately following the traumatic stressor. It may become manifest at any time following the exposure to such stressor(s).

Post-Traumatic Stress Disorder, as described in DSM-IV (APA, 1994), is "the development of characteristic symptoms following exposure to an extreme traumatic stressor." If an individual has not been exposed to a traumatic stressor, PTSD cannot be diagnosed as the causal agent of mental health disorder. In order to accurately conceptualize PTSD, it is necessary to clearly understand what "extreme traumatic stressor" means. As described in DSM-IV, a traumatic stressor must involve actual or threatened death or serious injury or other threat to one's physical integrity. Such events are not limited to those experienced directly, but can be witnessed or experienced vicariously.

In addition to having survived a traumatic event, a PTSD diagnosis under DSM-IV criteria requires that an individual exhibit symptoms from three categories: (a) re-experiencing, (b) avoidance/numbing, and (c) increased baseline physiological arousal. Re-experiencing symptoms include intrusive thoughts of the trauma, nightmares, flashbacks, and *trigger responses* (i.e., becoming distressed when a stimulus reminiscent of the trauma is encountered). Avoidance/numbing symptoms include avoiding situations reminiscent of the trauma, amnesia relating to part of the trauma, isolation from others, and a general feeling of emotional numbness. Arousal symptoms include insomnia, angry outbursts or irritability, and a general sense of jumpiness.

In studies among incarcerated populations, PTSS were found in approximately 48 percent of female inmates and 30 percent of male inmates (Baker & Alfonso, 2002). The diagnostic criteria of PTSS is underscored in the most recent edition: DSM-IV-TR (APA, 2000).

Research studies that examine extreme traumatic events that result in PTSD are numerous. For example, the tremendous and uncontrollable stress during U.S. Army survival training was found in some cases to lead to acute trauma and PTSD (Morgan, Hazlett, Wang, & Richardson, 2001). Many studies have been conducted on PTSD caused by combat, assault and rape, natural disasters, child abuse, kidnapping, family economic struggles, and school shootings (Foa, Riggs, & Gershuny, 1995; Kizer, 1996; Lorenz, Conger, Montague, & Wickrama, 1993; Schwarz & Kowalski, 1991). However, research has shown that reactions to traumatic experiences are temporary and mild for some, by comparison to the severe and lasting psychological distress reported by others (Figley, 1978; Port, Engdahl & Frazier, 2001; Solomon, 2001).

Breslau, Davis, and Andreski (1995) studied 1,200 members of a health maintenance organization and found that 19 percent of the sample reported having experienced traumatic events, and that a history of past exposure signaled an increase in liability in future exposure. Odds of exposure for males, and those with less than a college education, were found to be marginally significant. Early misconduct and family history of psychiatric disorder were also predictors of previous exposure. The study also noted that Blacks had higher exposure incidence compared to Whites in follow-up interviews. The authors concluded that PTSD-related traumatic events are not random; young adults, those with less education, and Blacks are more likely to be exposed to trauma and to develop PTSS (Breslau et al.).

Pre-Incarceration

Streetwise and Criminality

Pre-incarceration events and experiences shape some individuals to be streetwise and/or disposed to criminality. These elements may be related to adult incarceration as well as PTSS. In the general population, evidence suggests that those who have experienced adversity are more likely to engage in substance abuse and criminal behavior (Dembo et al., 1990; Dohrenwend, 2000; Logan, Walker, Staton, & Leukfeld, 2001). Adams (1992) conducted an extensive review of empirical research, reporting that individual characteristics and environmental factors affected prison adjustment, and that they are related to emotional disorders or disruptive behavior.

Profiles of prisoners who are involved in disciplinary issues in prisons indicate that they have experienced pre-prison problems in domestic, educational, and occupational endeavors; however, research on pre-incarceration criminal history shows mixed findings, and it remains unclear how these experiences affect prison adjustment (Adams, 1992). This study adds insight into the effect of pre-prison experiences upon prison adjustment, laying a foundation for analysis of the relationship between prison experiences and development of PTSS.

Guthrie (1999) reported that prisoners tend to come from economically and socially disadvantaged circumstances in which violence, family disruption, substance abuse, and other traumatic experiences are common. In a survey of male inmates, he found that subjects reported having experienced three times more traumatic events than noninstitutionalized comparison groups.

Researchers have noted that inmates enter prison with backgrounds and characteristics that affect their relationships with other inmates and correctional staff, as well as their ability to cope with anxiety and objective difficulties present in the prison environment (Hochstetler, Murphy and Simons, 2004; Gullone, Jones, & Cummins, 2000; Silverman & Vega, 1990; Verona, Patrick, & Joiner, 2001). Sykes (1958), in discussing the Importation Model, provides insight into the culture of prison. Sykes describes prison culture as the simultaneous interplay of personal characteristics and the conditions of confinement. It may be that pre-prison experiences not only lead to adult incarceration, but may also lead to PTSS prior to or following entry into prison.

On average, prisoners tend to have experienced previous psychological distress and disorders (Powell, Holt, & Fondacaro, 1997). For a combination of reasons that pertain to the etiology of emotional disorders, the efficacy of treatment interventions, and the stressful nature of prison environments, a history of psychological treatment may indicate a major risk factor for the onset of serious emotional difficulties in prison. Research indicates that approximately 20 percent of inmates have spent time in a mental health treatment facility, or reported mental illness (BJS, 1997). In a separate study, 86 percent of prisoners reported they had received at least one psychiatric diagnosis in their lifetime (Chiles, von Cleve, Jemelka, & Trupin, 1990). Other investigators have shown that prisoners have high rates of personality disorders (Davison, Leese, & Taylor, 2001), affective disorders, functional psychosis (Smith, O'Neal, Tobin, & Walshe, 1996), depression, PTSD (Powell et al., 1997; Brinded et al., 2001; Goff et al.,2007), and many other psychological problems (Hodgins & Cote, 1990).

Being streetwise and/or engaging in criminality may ultimately result in a life-guiding behavioral schema that an individual incorporates in dealing with an array of situational conditions in the prison environment. The following section investigates the possibility that being streetwise and involved in criminality prepare individuals for the transition from the streets to the "total institution" (Goffman, 1961) of prison.

Preparation for Prison

While some have found that pre-incarceration experiences may lead to psychological problems that can be exacerbated by incarceration, others have found that individual correlates and previous experiences may actually lead to more effective adjustment to the prison environment. Johnson (1976) reports that Black inmates are less susceptible to emotional disorders than are White inmates. Kessler (1979) explains the resilience to depression found among African Americans is a function of earlier and frequent exposure to stress. He explains that racial disparity and racism may insulate African Americans against stress in that they are forced by the environment to accommodate the associated stressors. Pre-prison lives of many Black inmates, that require survival in urban ghettos, may have trained them in street survival skills that are useful in prison. Exposure to the criminal justice system and inculcation into the "code of the street" (Anderson, 1999) may prepare individuals to better cope with the prison environment and thereby reduce the likelihood of developing PTSS as result of the prison experience.

Scholars have pointed out that a variety of life experiences train people in street survival skills, and that these skills can be used to an advantage in prison. Results indicate that state-raised youth, or persons who have spent the better part of their childhood and adolescence in institutions, may be better prepared for the prison environment through familiarity with institutional life (Bartollas, 1982; Irwin, 1970, 1980; Irwin & Cressey, 1962). Further, familiarity with the "code of the street" (Anderson, 1999) may prepare individuals for the strictures of the convict code.

Family and Negative Parenting

Juvenile delinquency has long been associated with family context. Jang and Smith (1997) studied the correlation between family relationships and delinquency. They analyzed the specific relationship between affective relationships, parental supervision, and their impact on delinquency. The study included 1,000 adolescents who were followed for 4-1/2 years until the end of their 11th and 12th grades. Interviews were conducted at 6-month intervals with the adolescents and their caretakers. Findings indicate that parental supervision had a significant negative relationship with delinquency, and while affective relations between parent and adolescent did not significantly influence delinquency, delinquency did negatively influence the affective child/parent relationship.

Chambers, Power, Loucks, and Swanson (2000) studied prison inmates and found strong associations between low parental care and low levels of self-esteem. They found diminished self-esteem to be associated with increased likelihood of future psychological distress, and they found that the prison experience amplified distress levels among these subjects. It was also found that low maternal care was related to poor peer relationships with inmates, which further exacerbated levels of psychological distress.

Dembo et al. (1990) found that a history of childhood physical abuse and/or sexual victimization results in youths who are at high risk for future deviant behavior, and that these factors may contribute to adult incarceration. It was also found that physical and sexual abuse leads to the development of PTSS (APA, 1994). These finding support a premise of the current research, that pre-prison experiences may cause PTSS prior to incarceration.

Incarceration

Psychological Consequences

Variation in inmates' accounts of their prison experiences and lasting psychological effects of incarceration are striking (Hochstetle, Murphy and Simons, 2004; Toch & Adams, 1989a; Toch, 1977). Even those who have served comparable sentences in the same facilities often have experiences that differ markedly (Hemmens & Marquart, 1999). Distress researchers concur that individual pre-event characteristics and post-event resources, in conjunction with the specific quality of exposure to potentially damaging experiences, significantly influence the impact of traumatic events on individuals (Benotsch et al., 2000; Breslau, Davis, & Andreski, 1995; Gold et al., 2000; Kessler et al., 1999; McFarlane, 1989).

Elements of incarceration may be traumatic and adjustment to the prison environment may be very difficult. Adams (1992) notes that prison maladjustment may lead to self-mutilation, suicide attempts, prison misbehavior, and emotional disorders. Examples of prison experiences that may be perceived as traumatic events include solitary confinement, victimization, witnessing victimization, fear of victimization, overcrowding, and exposure to disease. These events may lead to dissociative symptoms (to lose oneself) that may be associated with acute and uncontrollable stress (Morgan et al., 2001). It is reasonable to hypothesize that uncontrollable stress, which may result from the prison experience, may lead to the onset of PTSS.

Previous studies have concentrated more on the effects of incarceration on psychological distress and well-being than on the implications of developing PTSS. For example, Cooper and Berwick (2001) studied 171 male inmates serving different sentences. They analyzed the effects of incarceration on psychological distress in three groups of suicide-prone prisoners to determine if the combination of institutional and individual factors were related to levels of anxiety, depression, and psychological well-being. Findings showed that institutional hassles and worries associated with day-to-day living conditions, psychiatric history, guilt feelings, religious faith, lack of close friends outside prison, and tendencies not to take part in activities, were associated with high levels of distress. The present study builds upon this literature by analyzing the specific relationship between aspects of the prison experience and development of PTSS.

The Mentally Ill Offender

Ditton (1999) reports that over three-quarters of the prisoners deemed mentally ill had sentences prior to their present period of incarceration. Of this group over 30 percent of the males and 78 percent of the females reported prior physical or sexual abuse. Further, 61 percent of state prisoners and 41 percent of prisoners in local jails reported prior treatment for a mental condition. The Florida Corrections Commission Annual Report (1999) underscores the problematic relationship between the prison environment and mental health outcomes. It is indicated in the report that prison brutality and overcrowding can negatively affect inmates with no prior mental illness history. This finding supports a tenet of the present research that the prison experience itself may cause PTSS.

Research on mental health history of inmates indicates that those most vulnerable to psychological breakdown in prison are inmates with a history of emotional difficulties (Adams, 1992). Ditton (1999) reported that state prison inmates with a mental condition were more likely to be incarcerated for violent offenses than other inmates (53 percent compared to 46 percent). These inmates were also more likely to have been under the influence of alcohol and/or drugs (comorbidity) during the offense, and were twice as likely to have been homeless.

However, research has also found that even though the violent mentally ill offenders are a valid concern, this population is not nearly as big a problem as is usually portrayed in the media. Researchers tracked 337 mentally ill prisoners who were released from Washington State prisons in 1996 and 1997 (Lovell, Gagliardi, & Peterson, 2002). Persons with schizophrenia, major affective disorders, and borderline personality disorder made up most of the sample. Although charges for new crimes or supervision violation were common (70 percent), just 10 percent committed new felonies against persons, and 2 percent committed serious violent offenses (homicide, rape, first-degree robbery, or assault). The follow-up period for this study was 31 months. These findings underscore the challenge of post-incarceration reintegration faced by those suffering mental illness. Although 2 percent may be considered a rate high enough to justify allocation of resources for treatment and follow-up services on the grounds of public safety, emphasizing this danger to the public may only reinforce public fear of those suffering mental health challenges. This perception may discourage efforts to reach out to mentally ill offenders and keep them engaged in community mental health and other social support services.

Underscoring the need to treat the mentally ill offender, Brinded et al. (2001) reported findings of a New

Zealand prisoners study. The research used a random national sample of female and male inmates and compared findings to a representative community sample. Using diagnostic criteria, respondents were interviewed to determine DSM-IV diagnoses of psychiatric disorders. Findings showed a markedly elevated prevalence rate for major mental disorders in the prison sample, as compared to the community sample. The study found high levels of substance misuse, psychotic disorders, major depression, bipolar disorder, compulsive disorder, and PTSS within the inmate sample.

PTSS as Precursor

PTSS may be linked to criminal behavior, in that symptoms may lead to offenses that can be connected to previously experienced extreme trauma. For example, PTSS may result in criminal actions such as sudden outbursts of violent behavior. Environmental conditions that are similar to those which existed at the time of the trauma can induce flashback behavior. The presence of PTSS may therefore be the cause of crime in certain instances, and some prisoners may have acquired these symptoms prior to incarceration.

Of specific concern are incarcerated military veterans who may have engaged in criminal behavior as civilians. It may be that PTSS acquired in military service precipitated their criminal actions (Ex-Services Mental Welfare Society, 2003). Thus, those having served in defense of their country may experience the indirect consequence of PTSS acquired in the military that then contributed to post-military incarceration (Greenburg & Rosencheck, 2009).

Environmental Factors

Studies have investigated prison physical characteristics and security levels for effects on adjustment. Studies of the effects of noise levels, temperature, and aesthetics have been inconclusive since findings show mixed results; however, it has been concluded that in high-security settings, inmate adjustment is related to cell satisfaction, which may be related to feelings of safety, as well as control over lighting, heating, and ventilation. Prisons that attend to order, security, and safety, were found to exhibit less violence and more program participation (Adams, 1992). Lower levels of violence within the prison environment and increased levels of program participation may reduce the likelihood of inmates' developing PTSS as result of the incarceration experience.

The Inmate Economy

The illegitimate inmate economy is driven by force, fear, tobacco, drugs/alcohol, and sex (Cooperstein, 2001). There are specific rules that govern the exchange of contraband in the prison setting. For example, a fundamental rule is two-for-one. If an individual borrows a pack of cigarettes, the exchange rate need not be discussed. It is common knowledge that the borrower will have to repay two packs for the one borrowed.

Given the restrictive nature of the prison environment, cost of contraband is high and prices widely known. It is common within the inmate economy for a *pin joint* (a very thin marijuana cigarette) to command a price of 10 dollars, a carton of cigarettes, or three books of stamps. In addition, sexual favors may be exchanged for contraband.

At the individual level, involvement in the inmate economy may be very dangerous. If an individual borrows and fails to repay, the convict code requires swift and severe recompense. Failure to repay may result in physical attack and victimization. Additionally, victimization may be the source of further victimization. The victimized individual may be perceived as weak and thus may be considered a suitable target for victimization by other prisoners. Further, the stress associated with the act of participating in the inmate economy may reach the level of traumatic event independent of victimization and result in development of PTSS.

At the institutional level, the inmate economy may affect the stability of the prison environment. Sudden changes in the level of contraband may have economic effects that have the potential to affect the stability of the community of prisoners. There are no realistic substitutes for most of the contraband goods and services marketed in prison, making the demand for those goods and services highly price sensitive. If the supply of contraband is successfully cut, the price levels increase, and the desired consumption of contraband decreases. Given the rise in cost, prisoners may increase their illegitimate income through whatever means available in an effort to meet their consumption needs, for example by victimizing other prisoners. This may lead to an increase in criminal activity such as extortion and theft.

The high price for illegal services results in increased profits to suppliers. Other prisoners seeing the profits made by suppliers may attempt to enter the supply market. The attempt of contraband dealers to encroach on the territory of other suppliers may be met with violence. Thus, a sudden reduction in the supply of contraband may increase the potential for instability, disorder, and violence in the prison community, thereby increasing the potential for individual victimization. The stress associated with participation in the inmate economy may itself lead to onset of PTSS independent of actual victimization.

The Convict Code

The *convict code* is a set of rules that is clearly delineated, verbalized, and internalized. The code defines consequential meanings of situations and actions. It is a set of norms, rules, and values that define prison culture. The convict code is the foundation for what has been described as the "subculture of prison" (Wieder, 2001; Sykes & Messinger, 1960).

The convict code consists of clearly defined maxims that govern interaction. There is agreement on the elements that constitute the convict code, although some institutional variation on how the code is implemented exists between institutions. This discussion covers the basic components of the convict code. A detailed discussion of the discrete elements contained in the convict code is subject for a study unto itself.

It is important to understand the convict code, for violation of the norms and values of the code carry consequences. Whereas consequences of violating the convict code may induce stress, the convict code itself may induce high levels of stress. Aside from the actual consequences of violating the convict code, the potential for consequences associated with code violation are constant. This stress is present independent of actual consequences, and for some, traumatic. Therefore, the stress associated with the convict code itself may cause PTSS.

A maxim of the convict code is Do not snitch (inform): "I don't know anything about anything." Other elements of the convict code include, but are not limited to:

- Do not cop out (admitting guilt)
- Do not take advantage of other prisoners (whereas this rule is clearly articulated, more accurately this rule states do not take advantage of other prisoners who are your "home boys" or close associates)
- Share what you have for we are all in this hellhole together
- You watch my back and I'll watch yours
- Do not inquire about other prisoners' personal business
- Do your own time
- Do not trust staff or prison officials for they are the enemy (be a stand-up con)
- Be polite and respectful (don't "dis" anyone); however, a prisoner must straddle the line of being polite and respectful without showing undue deference that may be perceived as weakness

Learned Helplessness

Certain objective conditions, such as powerlessness and dependency, create a sense of detachment from one's own actions and outcomes that people find demoralizing and distressing (Horwitz & Scheid, 1999; Mirowsky & Ross, 1999). The prison experience is an extreme example of powerlessness and dependency, a setting in which virtually all aspects of life are controlled. Goodstein, MacKenzie, and Shortland (1984) describe the outcome of excessive control as "learned helplessness." Seligman (1975) describes learned helplessness as the withdrawal of effort and feelings of dejection that accompany exposure to inescapable, uncontrollable negative stimuli.

Learned helplessness acquired in prison may pose serious challenges for society when prisoners are released. Given current incarceration policies, where sentences run for decades, released prisoners face the transition from being controlled, to taking control of their daily lives. The released prisoner is suddenly faced with aspects of daily life such as shopping, balancing a checkbook, and getting a job, activities which were completely controlled in the prison setting. For some prisoners who become institutionalized, making the transition from learned helpless to self-efficacy will be extremely difficult, and for others, impossible. Such individuals will ultimately recidivate and return to the total institution of prison. The trauma of reintegration for those who develop learned helplessness as result of the total institution of prison may cause PTSS for certain individuals.

Victimization

The General Population

Studies of post-crime distress due to criminal victimization have been conducted among the general population. Even a single nonviolent offense committed against free citizens can have lasting psychological consequences and affect future perception of security (Davis, Taylor, & Lurigio, 1996; Denkers & Winkel, 1997; Hraba, Lorenz, Pechacova, & Bao, 1999; Norris & Kaniasty, 1994). Several studies have shown that household burglary significantly predicts depressive symptoms and psychological difficulties for victims, and that these symptoms often last for months (Cabellero, Ramos, & Saltijeral, 2000; Beaton, Cook, Cavanaugh, & Harrington, 2000).

Davis, Taylor, and Lurigio (1996) studied postcrime psychological distress among victims of burglary, robbery, and nonsexual assault. Interviews that took place 1 month following the incident, and again 3 months later, provide relevant data. Demographic characteristics and victim perceptions accounted for the greatest amount of variance in outcomes. Given that victimization occurs more frequently in the prison population, and that many prisoners are already psychologically vulnerable, it is reasonable to hypothesize that prison victimization may lead to PTSS at higher levels than in the general population.

The Prison Experience

Given the effects of criminal victimization in the general population, there is reason to believe that victimization in prison affects prisoners' distress levels, especially when victimization is repeated (Hochstetler, Murphy and Simons, 2004). Therefore, it is reasonable to hypothesize that in-prison victimization may reach the traumatic level required to induce PTSS.

Most investigators of victimization in prison focused solely on violent victimization. The focus, while understandable, obscures the toll that nonviolent or routine criminal victimization may have on inmates (O'Donnell & Edgar, 1998). Numerous studies find that some inmates are viewed as easy targets. These vulnerable prisoners endure repeated harassment through theft, robbery, vandalism, fraud, and other offenses, often with the threat of violence underlying all of the crimes (O'Donnell & Edgar; Sykes, 1958; Toch, 1992). The repeated exposure to nonviolent victimization may lead to development of PTSS.

Maitland and Sluder (1996) investigated inmate victimization in a Midwest prison. The authors report a relationship between victimization and associated individual, psychological, social, and institutional variables. Wooldredge (1998) reports that inmate-on-inmate crime is a serious type of victimization and personal characteristics of lifestyle traits predispose certain individuals to be victimized. A premise of this study is that as in-prison victimization increases, likelihood of developing PTSS increases.

Fear of crime inside correctional facilities leads to fear of victimization (McCorkle, 1992, 1993a, 1993b; Wright,

1991). In a study of 300 inmates from a maximum-security facility in Tennessee, McCorkle (1993b) found a higher rate of fear inside the prison compared to what has been documented in the free world. Higher levels of fear inside the prison were found to be associated with prisoners who were young, socially isolated, and more likely to be a frequent target of victimization. While long-term exposure to prison conditions is not damaging to inmates in a uniform way, there is evidence that these conditions tend to produce psychological disturbances for some (Adams, 1992).

Hemmens's (1999) research supports previous findings that inmates experience fear of violence and victimization in prison. A survey of 775 adult male inmates analyzed the effects of race, ethnicity, and prior criminal history on reports of fear. Findings showed that race/ethnicity were not factors, but age was related to perceptions of violence and victimization in prison. Younger prisoners reported higher levels of fear and were more likely to describe prison as a dangerous place.

O'Donnell and Edgar (1998) studied adult male prisoners to determine a view of day-to-day victimization in prison. Their findings indicate that younger prisoners were victimized more than older offenders. For the group of young prisoners, verbal abuse was most common, followed by threats and assaults. A premise of this study is that the variable age first incarcerated is negatively related to victimization and fear of victimization.

A survey of inmates in three Ohio prisons found that 50 percent had been victims of a crime in prison, and 10 percent had been assaulted in the previous 6 months of their period of incarceration (Wooldredge,

1994). Official records of inmates in 36 New York facilities revealed that 10 percent were cited for assault in a 3-year period; 13 percent for theft; and 12 percent for vandalism (Wooldredge and Carboneau, 1998). However, what must be borne in mind is that these figures represent only officially recorded offenses. Therefore, one can only speculate as to the magnitude of actual prisoner victimization as well as to the actual number of offenses committed. The unreported incidents represent the dark figure of crime that is actually occurring within the prison environment.

Drawing upon research from the general population, victimization has been shown to lead to PTSS (Schiff, El-Bassell, Engstrtom, & Gilbert, 2002; Yap & Devilly, 2004). Given that victimization rates are higher in the prison environment than in the general population, it is reasonable to hypothesize that the prison experience itself may lead to higher incidence of PTSS.

Prison Domain–Specific Lifestyle Theory

A place-specific application of lifestyle theory is implemented as a theoretical perspective to frame the hypotheses analyzed in this study (Wooldredge, 1994, 1998, 1999). Building upon opportunity theories, most notably routine activities theory (Cohen & Felson, 1979) and lifestyle/exposure theory (Hindelang et al., 1978), the prison domain–specific application of lifestyle theory offers one explanation for variation of victimization within the prison environment. Whereas the following discussion focuses on victimization, the same tenets hold true for participation in the inmate economy, witnessing victimization, and adherence to the convict code.

Spatial and temporal elements of individual victimization, defined under the rubric "place of crime" (Eck & Weisburd, 1995) help explain why some places and individuals become targets for victimization. Wooldredge (1998) postulates that victimization risk is influenced by lifestyle patterns or daily activities within the prison setting that either increase or decrease victimization opportunities. Thus, there are high-risk activities, locations, and times that can be noted within the correctional institution.

"Victimization is not evenly distributed randomly across time and space—there are high risk locations and high risk periods" (Garofalo, 1987, p. 26). Such conditions are prevalent in the prison environment, therefore it is reasonable to hypothesize those high-risk conditions in the prison setting lead to victimization, and that victimization may in turn lead to PTSS.

Within the framework of lifestyle theory, individuals are viewed as either engaging in activities that increase or decrease interactions with potential victimizers. Patterns of activities may influence exposure to situations that are at high risk for victimization. Thus, inmates who spend more time each day in structured activities that are legitimate may have a lower likelihood of being victimized. Alternatively, less structured activities are less supervised and may lead to higher levels of victimization (Wooldredge, 1998).

While participation in less structured activities may lead to victimization, other aspects of the correctional institution add to this risk. Physical boundaries place people in close proximity that influence vulnerability as well. Individuals may be placed in close contact with others who are dissimilar to themselves and this may increase chances of victimization.

Studies have shown demographic and background variables predict the likelihood of physical assault in the prison environment. Some types of inmates appear to be more prone to victimization, and lifestyle factors appear to be related to this outcome (Wooldredge, 1998). Research has shown that younger inmates are more likely to suffer multiple forms of victimization and that the victimization of physical assault is more likely to occur among Whites, more educated inmates, and those incarcerated for property offenses (C. E. Silberman, 1995; M. Silberman, 1995).

Race—although possibly confounded with urban poverty and income—and age, have also been associated with prison adjustment (Adams, 1992; Guthrie, 1999). Although the interpretation of these findings may be controversial, many explanations of racial differences focus on subcultural differences, while explanations of age differences focus on processes of learning and maturation. Research indicates that Black inmates tend to be more unruly than White prisoners, as well as younger, inmates tend to be more prone to victimization (Fuller & Orsagh, 1977; Toch, 1977).

Hypotheses

Routine activities theory (Cohen & Felson, 1979) and lifestyle/exposure theory (Hindelang et al., 1978) suggest that lifestyle influences likelihood of victimization, as well as development of attitudes and activity patterns that may contribute to victimization. Wooldredge (1994, 1998, 1999) expands upon routine activities theory and lifestyle/exposure theory by analyzing prison domain–specific characteristics that may lead to victimization. These theoretical foundations, in conjunction with findings in the literature, guide formation of hypotheses analyzed in this study.

Hypothesis 1

Pre-prison experiences affect adjustment to prison in the manner described below.

Model 1: Effect of Pre-Prison Variables on Inmate Economy

1.1a) As measures of streetwise increase, the likelihood of participation in the inmate economy increases.

1.1b) As measures of pre-prison criminality increase, the likelihood of participation in the inmate economy increases.

1.1c) As measures of frequency in the system increase, the likelihood of participation in the inmate economy increases.

1.1d) As measures of Negative Parenting increase, the likelihood of participation in the inmate economy increases.

Model 2: Effect of Pre-Prison Variables on In-Prison Victimization

1.2a) As measures of streetwise increase, the likelihood of in-prison victimization increases.

1.2b) As measures of pre-prison criminality increase, the likelihood of in-prison victimization increases.

1.2c) As measures of frequency in the system increase, the likelihood of in-prison victimization increases.

1.2d) As measures of negative parenting increase, the likelihood of in-prison victimization increases.

Model 3: Effect of Pre-Prison variables on Witness Victimization

1.3a) As measures of streetwise increase, the likelihood of in-prison witness victimization increases.

1.3b) As measures of pre-prison criminality increase, likelihood of in-prison witness victimization increases.

1.3c) As measures of frequency in the system increase, likelihood of in-prison witness victimization increases.

1.3d) As measures of negative parenting increase, the likelihood of in-prison witness victimization increases.

Model 4: Effect of Pre-Prison Variables on Adherence to the Convict Code

1.4a) As measures of streetwise increase, the likelihood of adherence to the convict code increases.

1.4b) As measures of pre-prison criminality increase, the likelihood of adherence to the convict code increases.

1.4c) As measures of frequency in the system increase, likelihood of adherence to the convict code increases.

1.4d) As measures of negative parenting increase, likelihood of adherence to the convict code increases.

Hypothesis 2

Prison experiences, as described below, increase the likelihood of developing PTSS as result of the prison experience.

2.1) As measures of participation in the inmate economy increase, the likelihood of developing post-traumatic stress symptoms increases.

2.2) As measures of in-prison victimization increase, the likelihood of developing post-traumatic stress symptoms increases.

2.3) As measures of in-prison witness victimization increase, the likelihood of developing post-traumatic stress symptoms increases.

2.4) As measures of adherence to the convict code increase, the likelihood of developing post-traumatic stress symptoms increases.

Hypothesis 3

Pre-prison experiences, as described below, increase the likelihood of developing PTSS independent of the prison experience.

3.1) As measures of streetwise increase, the likelihood of developing PTSS independent of the prison experience increases.

3.2) As measures of pre-prison criminality increases, likelihood of developing PTSS independent of the prison experience increases.

3.3) As measures of frequency in the system increase, the likelihood of developing PTSS independent of the prison experience increases.

3.4) As measures of pre-prison negative parenting increase, the likelihood of developing PTSS independent of the prison experience increases.

Hypothesis 4: Fully Recursive Model

To gain further insight into stressors that may lead to the development of PTSS, analysis of the relationship between pre-prison and in-prison independent variables implemented in this study and the development of PTSS, is provided. This analysis further enlightens the analysis of potential stressors that may result in PTSS.

Chapter 3. Methodology

This chapter includes a general description of the research approach, a discussion of the sample from which the data were collected, a discussion of data collection procedures, a discussion of potential enhancement of internal validity, discussion of measures, and a discussion of symptoms data versus clinical diagnosis.

Research Approach

The focus of this research is on the analysis of relationships between pre-prison experiences and adjustment to the prison environment, in-prison experiences and onset of PTSS, and between pre-prison experiences and onset of PTSS, independent of the incarceration experience. Also analyzed is a combination of both pre-prison and in-prison independent variables and their relationship to development of PTSS. These relationships lay a foundation for a discussion of the implications associated with prisoners who return to the community experiencing PTSS.

Population Sample

The population from which the sample was drawn consisted of all persons meeting the following criteria: (a) men sentenced to incarceration in prison in a Midwestern state; (b) men who were incarcerated and served their sentence; (c) men who were transferred from prison to a work release facility; (d) men who had been in the work release program for 6 months or less at the time of interview and who were within a few months of being released to less restrictive community supervision.

The sample of this population was drawn from the work release residents at a number of work release facilities located in a state in the Midwest United States. Of the 480 work release residents at the facilities, 208 who met the four criteria agreed to participate in the data collection. While the sample from which the data were collected was a nonprobability convenience sample, the high proportion (43.3 percent) of the total work release population participating in the data collection may enhance the internal validity of the data and corresponding findings.

The participants did not differ significantly from the general prison populations of the facilities visited or from released prisoners in the state. The state-level data indicate that the sample is similar to released inmates on age (sample 32 years old; population 31), race (sample 61 percent White; population 72 percent White), offense type (sample 28 percent violent, 22 percent drug; population 28 percent violent, 22 percent drug), and time served (sample 38 months; population 29 months; Hochstetler,

Murphy & Simons, 2004). Inmate composition varies by state, and imprisonment differs within states and between states. Standard cautions for a convenience sample should be taken in interpreting and generalizing from this study's findings.

Data Collection Procedures

In effort to recruit respondents, brochures announcing the research project were posted in the work release facilities a week in advance, and a sign-up sheet was provided at each facility's front desk. The brochures promised that the information in the study was confidential and reassured residents of the right to refuse any question. Participants were paid $30.00 for their efforts.

The data were collected at work release facilities in a Midwest state where the members of the research sample were residents. The survey questionnaires were administered in small groups with the researcher present to answer respondent questions. Confidentiality of respondent's identity and individual responses was protected. Time required for survey completion ranged from 1 to 2 hours.

Researcher-Respondent Interaction: Convict Criminology

The author has personal experience in common with the respondents since he had spent 5-1/2 years confined in the Federal Bureau of Prisons followed by 4 years supervised release. The authors' experience within the prison system, and the potential effect of this experience on the data's internal validity, need be discussed.

The researcher shared his prison experience with the respondents and provided for respondent review a copy of the researcher's pre-sentence investigation report (PSI). It appeared the respondents developed a trusting relationship with the author predicated upon their common prison experience. The researcher noted the time and effort put forth by the respondents in completing the survey instrument and suggests that this thoughtful effort may be linked to the shared prison experience. However, this element of the data collection procedures cannot be easily replicated and therefore its reliability may be suspect.

After observing the phenomena of a trusting relationship between researcher and respondents, the researcher asked an academic colleague to participate in several of the data collection sessions. Through independent observation, the associate researcher noted the same trusting interaction between the primary researcher and respondents. However, it is important to note that the associate researcher questioned the importance and impact of the relationship between respondent and researcher as related to internal validity.

The interaction between author and respondent goes to the debate that has been ongoing within the academy: emics and etics, (Headland, Pike, & Harris, 1990; Murphy, 2007) the insider versus outsider, the subjective versus the objective. The question raised within the emics and etics dichotomy queries: If a researcher has domain-specific experience in common with the respondents, does that experience lead to better research than if the shared commonality did not exist? For example, is it possible for a researcher who is White to conduct fruitful inquiry into issues salient to African Americans? Can a man conduct research within the context of a feminist perspective? Is prison-related research conducted by a researcher with prison experience more insightful than research conducted by investigators who do not have personal experience in the correctional system?

Given the body of insightful research produced by investigators who do not have domain-specific personal experience, the answer to the question raised indicates that this type of personal experience is not necessarily required. However, if viewed through the lens of the Weberian ideal type, if all skills and dimensions were equal, yet one researcher had domain-specific personal experience, it may be that the individual with the personal experience has advantage. Clearly, the world is not structured as an ideal type; therefore, the author of the present study suggests the possibility that his personal prison experience and his shared understanding of the convict code may have fostered a positive interaction with the respondents and thereby elicited thoughtful responses. It may be that the researcher was viewed as an insider predicated upon personal experience shared with the respondents. However, the researcher underscores that this may be a subjective interpretation and is therefore subject to standard cautions.

Verification Questions

A second measure contained in survey construction that allows for measuring an indication of accuracy in reading and answering the survey questions were two verification questions placed within the body of the questionnaire. For these questions, the respondent was asked to check a specified option in the response set. The purpose of these questions was to get a quantifiable indication that the respondents were reading the questions closely. Of the 208 respondents, only two did not select the required response for these two questions. Inclusion or exclusion of these participants had no significant effect on findings.

Measures

Control Variables

Based on previous literature, this study accounts for the effect of race, education, and age first incarcerated. For the purpose of analysis, race is dummy coded 1 = White and 0 = other. Race is thought to affect likelihood of incarceration and several aspects of prison adjustment. Blacks are incarcerated at a rate of 3,161 per 100,000, Hispanics at a rate of 1,200 per 100,000, and Whites at a rate of 487 per 100,000 (BJS, 2009a; Sentencing Project, 2010).

Previous literature indicates that level of education is related to incarceration and adjustment to prison. Ryan, Davis, and Yang (2001) indicate that education is negatively related to incarceration, and Greene et al. (2000) report that those with higher levels of education are more likely to be victimized in prison than are those with lower levels of education.

Hemmens (1999) reports that younger prisoners

reported higher levels of fear and were more likely to describe prison as a dangerous place. O'Donnell and Edgar (1998) report that younger inmates are more likely to be victimized than are older inmates.

Variable Construction

Streetwise

Streetwise (Cronbach's alpha = .72) incorporates a series of questions designed to capture attitudes acquired prior to incarceration that may affect prison adjustment. Implementing a Likert-type scale from 1 (*strongly disagree*) to 4 (*strongly agree*), items measured the respondent's streetwise in terms of (Appendix 1): having a reputation of being a tough guy (M = 2.60; SD = .83); being streetwise (M = 3.12; SD = .71); and being accustomed to dealing with streetwise people (M = 3.13; SD = .77).

Pre-Prison Criminality

The variable pre-prison criminality (Cronbach's alpha = .74) is designed to capture pre-prison criminality and activities that may be related to adult incarceration, and that may influence adjustment to the prison environment. The respondents completed an adult index of criminal behavior adapted from the National Youth Survey (Elliot, Juizinga, & Ageton, 1985; Elliot, Juizinga, & Menard, 1989). The major modification involved substituting adult deviant acts for the delinquent behavior included in the adolescent instrument. The response categories include:

1 (*never*), 2 (*about 1-2 times*), 3 (*about once a month*), 4 (*about once a week*), 5 (*2-3 times per week or more*). Survey items probed pre-prison criminality such as (Appendix 1): breaking the law on a regular basis (M = 2.75; SD = .84); carrying a weapon (M = 2.26; SD = 1.53); and being involved in fights (M = 1.83; SD = .92).

Frequency in the System

The variable frequency in the System (Cronbach's alpha = .63) is designed to measure involvement with the criminal justice system. Involvement in the system may be related to prison adjustment, which in turn may be related to development of PTSS as result of the prison experience. Response categories include:1 (*1 time*), 2 (*2 times*), 3 (*3-5 times*), 4 (*6-10 times*), 5 (*11 or more times*). Respondents were asked (Appendix 1): How many times have you been arrested? (M = 4.03, SD = 1.11); How many times have you been to prison? (M = 2.02, SD = .90).

Negative Parenting

The negative parenting index is designed to measure aspects of child-parent interactions that could negatively impact an individual during the formative years of childhood. Negative parenting may affect prison adjustment or may contribute to PTSS independent of the prison experience. The negative parenting index was derived from the National Youth Survey (Elliot et al., 1985; Elliot et al., 1989) and includes response categories:1 (*always*), 2 (*almost always*), 3 (*fairly often*), 4 (*about half the time*), 5 (*not too often*), 6 (*almost never*), and 7 (*never*).

Respondents were asked 8 questions probing areas such as: How often in a typical month during grade school or junior high did your parent, parents, or guardian ... (Appendix 1): hit, push, grab, or shove you? ($M = 5.23$, $SD = 1.61$); insult or swear at you? ($M = 4.89$, $SD = 1.79$); threaten to hurt you by hitting you with their fist or something else? ($M = 5.18$, $SD = 1.79$); When you did something wrong, how often did your parent, parents, guardian slap you in the face or spank you with a paddle, belt, or some other object? ($M = 4.31$; $SD = 1.92$).

Participation in the Inmate Economy

The in-prison variables are designed to capture elements of the incarceration experience that may be influenced by pre-prison variables. Also, the in-prison variables are used to predict development of PTSS as result of the prison experience. The variable participation in the inmate economy (Cronbach's alpha = .69) is designed to capture an element of prison culture that may cause traumatic stress and result in the onset of PTSS. The inmate economy index was derived from topics discussed in the literature (Cooperstein, 2001) and the author's personal experience. Response categories ranged from: 1 (*never*), 2 (*about 1-2 times*), 3 (*about once a month*), 4 (*about once a week*), 5 (*2-3 times per week or more*). Questions asked include (Appendix 1): How often did you loan out goods for a profit? ($M = 2.48$; $SD = 1.43$); How often did you pay others to do work for you? ($M = 1.54$; $SD = .95$).

In one sense, prison is the great equalizer. Whether rich or poor, an individual is limited to $150 per month for commissary goods. The questions contained in the inmate economy index probe participation in the contraband economy of prison. Loaning out goods for a profit implies that an individual has accumulated surplus goods. Paying others to do work implies the same. The means by which individuals accumulate goods for loan or accumulate goods to pay others to do work is typically via illegal activity in the inmate economy.

Victimization

The variable victimization probes the respondents experience with different forms of victimization they may have experienced while incarcerated. Respondents completed an index of victimization adapted from the University of Michigan Composite International Diagnostic Index (UM-CIDI Victimization Scale Section). The major modification of the scale involved substituting prison domain specific sources of victimization for sources of victimization encountered in the general population. The response categories ranged from: 1 (*never*), 2 (*about 1-2 times*), 3 (*about once a month*), 4 (*about once a week*), 5 (*2-3 times per week or more*). The respondents were asked to indicate (Appendix 2): How often was something of yours stolen or vandalized? ($M = 2.48$; $SD = 1.43$); How often did another prisoner con you or scam you out of property or commissary? ($M = 1.54$; $SD = .68$); How often was personal property taken by use of force or intimidation? ($M = 1.12$; $SD = .41$); How often were you threatened with violence? ($M = 1.8$; $SD = .88$); How often were you assaulted with a weapon? ($M = 1.56$; $SD = .38$).

Witness Victimization

The variable witnessing victimization is designed to capture events that the literature indicates as a stressor that is common in the prison environment which may result in of PTSS (Cronbach's alpha = .83). The response categories ranged from: 1 (*never*), 2 (*about 1-2 times*), 3 (*about once a month*), 4 (*about once a week*), 5 (*2-3 times per week or more*). The respondents indicated (Appendix 2) how often they: saw another prisoner seriously injured (M = 2.11; SD = .93); saw another prisoner killed (M = 1.10; SD = .36); witnessed another prisoner's property being stolen or vandalized (M = 2.20; SD = 1.06); were aware of another prisoner being raped (M = 1.53; SD = .76); witnessed another prisoner being assaulted with a weapon (M = 1.72; SD = .82); witnessed other prisoners involved in fights (M = 2.80; SD = 1.09).

Convict Code

The variable adherence to the convict code (Cronbach's alpha = .75) is designed to capture an element of prison culture that may increase the likelihood of developing PTSS as result of the prison experience. The convict code measure was derived from issues discussed in the literature (Wieder, 2001) and the author's personal experience. Responses range from 1 (*strongly disagree*) to 4 (*strongly agree*). The items used to construct the variable adherence to the convict code include (Appendix 3) asked respondents to rate: confidence that a friend or associate would watch their back (M = 3.00; SD = .83); their regularly watching a friend's or associate's back

(M = 2.97; SD .83); their agreement with the statement, "I lived by the convict code" (M = 3.00; SD = .79).

Post-Traumatic Stress Symptoms

The variable PTSS (Cronbach's alpha = .90) was derived from the UM-CIDI Post Traumatic Stress Diagnostic Scale (Wittchen, Kessler, & Abelson, 1995). It is designed to measure PTSS that may develop as a result of the prison experience. A discussion of symptoms criteria versus diagnostic criteria follows. The response categories include: 1 (*yes*), 2 (*no*), and 3 (*don't know*). Respondents were asked questions such as (Appendix 3): Did you ever get very upset when you were in a situation that reminded you of the event? (M = .35, SD = .48); Did you develop a memory blank so that you could not remember certain things about the event? (M = .15, SD = .35)); Did you have more trouble concentrating than is usual? (M = .29, SD = .45).

Post-Traumatic Stress: Symptoms vs. Diagnostic Criteria

The present study incorporates 17 questions contained in the General Anxiety Disorder index section (GAD) of the UM-CIDI Post Traumatic Stress Diagnostic Scale. These questions are designed to measure Post Traumatic Stress Disorder criteria (Appendix 3). The UM-CIDI is a modified version of the Composite International Diagnostic Interview (CIDI) used in the U.S. National Comorbidity Survey (NCS; Wittchen et al., 1995). The NCS administered the CIDI to a nationally representative sample of 8,098 respondents in the age range 15 to 44.

It need be noted that the time dimensions used in the administration of the UM-CIDI were not included in this study. Time dimensions measured in the clinical diagnosis of mental health disorder include point of symptoms onset, duration of symptoms, and point of symptoms termination. Also included in a clinical diagnosis are measures of symptoms frequency and intensity. The present study implements post-traumatic stress symptoms (PTSS) measures rather than diagnostic criteria.

This study measures PTSS and the findings do not necessarily indicate the presence of a clinical diagnosis of post-traumatic stress disorder. The symptoms measures address a continuum of indices, which provides information relevant to the level of mental distress; whereas diagnostic criteria provide a dichotomized diagnosis of presence or absence of mental illness. In the present study respondents were asked to keep in mind the most traumatic event they experienced during their period of incarceration while answering the post-traumatic stress questions. Therefore, the approach used in the present study implements symptoms analysis and not clinical diagnosis.

Symptoms-based measures are beneficial in the study of the social epidemiology of mental health issues. Such measures are designed to be administered to large groups, and may be administered by laypersons. Compared to measures of diagnostic criteria, symptoms measures provide a mechanism to collect data from large samples at a relatively low cost.

Researchers have found strong correlation between symptoms-based measures and clinical diagnosis

(Peters, Andrews, Cottler, & Chatterji, 1996). Radloff (1977), for example, compared the findings of symptoms measures to diagnostic measures, finding high reliability and validity in the symptoms measurement included in the Center of Epidemiology Studies Depression Index when compared to measures of clinical diagnosis.

Aneshensel (1999) used symptoms criteria to examine the relationship between aspects of social structure and mental health disorders. In a similar fashion, the present study uses symptoms criteria to gain insight into the relationship between aspects of the incarceration experience and onset of PTSS. This approach, and the information gained, may be useful to clinicians in diagnosing individual prisoners who suffer PTSS. Also, the information may be useful in developing prison programs to address elements of the incarceration experience that are related to development of PTSS.

However, researchers have identified problems associated with the implementation of symptoms criteria. Aneshensel (1999) reported that a symptoms scale confounded acute and chronic stressors. Vega and Rumbaut (1991) reported social bias in the Center for Epidemiologic Studies–Depression Index (CES-D) symptoms measure. Their findings indicate that Blacks consistently show higher levels of depression compared to other racial groups, after controlling for class, education, and employment. The racial bias findings of Vega and Rumbaut were contradicted by the findings of the Detroit Area Study (Williams et al., 1997) who found that impoverished Blacks scored lower on the depression index than did comparable Whites. Therefore, standard caution is suggested when reviewing symptoms measures.

Chapter 4. Analysis

The present study uses zero-order correlation, and multiple regression analysis to test the significance, direction, and strength of the relationships between variables. Variables used in the present study are delineated in Appendices 1 through 4.

Zero-Order Correlation

Exploratory analysis of variable association reveals that: (a) with the exception of race and negative parenting, significant correlations exist between streetwise and the remaining variables analyzed in this study; (b) with the exception of education, pre-prison criminality is significantly correlated with all other variables; (c) with the exception of education, victimization, and PTSS, frequency in the system is significantly correlated with the remaining variables; (d) a significant relationship exists between negative parenting and inmate economy, victimization, witness victimization, and PTSS; (e) with exception of race and education, participation in the inmate economy is significantly related to the remainder of the variables; (f) a significant relationship exists between victimization and streetwise, pre-prison criminality, negative parenting, inmate economy, witness victimization, and PTSS; (g) a significant relationship exists between convict code and age first prison, streetwise, pre-prison criminality, frequency in system, inmate economy, and witness victimization; (h) a significant relationship exists between PTSS and streetwise, pre-prison criminality, negative parenting, inmate economy, victimization, and witness victimization (Table 4.1).

Multicollinearity

When using multiple variables that represent individualized characteristics of lifestyle and psychological measures, multicollinearity is always a concern and requires testing to determine if the independent variables are highly correlated. Because the results of the correlation analysis indicate that some of the independent variables were highly correlated an analysis of multicollinearity was performed.

There are varying approaches to detecting multicollinearity. Gujarati (1988) suggests that if the zero-order correlation coefficient is .80 or above, then multicollinearity is a serious problem (see also Bohrnstedt & Knoke, 1994). Other authors, however, use a more stringent indicator of multicollinearity and cite a correlation coefficient greater than .50 (Bohrnstedt & Knoke). In this study one correlation coefficient above .50 was detected among the independent variables: a correlation

Table 4.1 Zero-Order Correlations

	Race	Ed.	Age First Prison	Pre-Prison Strtws	Pre-Prison Crim.	Freq. System	Neg. Parent	Inmate Econ.	Victim	Witness Victim	Con. Code	PTSS
Race	1.00											
Education	.13	1.00										
Age First Prison	.12	.10	1.00									
Pre-Prison Streetwise	−.04	−.14*	−.34**	1.00								
Pre-Prison Criminality	−.19**	−.14	−.43**	.51**	1.00							
Frequency in System	.15*	.02	−.20**	.32**	.17*	1.00						
Negative Parenting	.09	−.01	−.11	.13	.15*	.22**	1.00					
Inmate Economy	−.08	−.04	−.34**	.32**	.57**	.20**	.22**	1.00				
Victimization	.13	−.05	−.14	.15*	.25**	.03	.32**	.30**	1.00			
Witness Victimization	−.08	−.11	−.43**	.44**	.55**	.17*	.19**	.44**	.41**	1.00		
Convict Code	.07	.02	−.32**	.53**	.37**	.20**	.07	.35**	.13	.40**	1.00	
PTSS	.04	−.03	−.05	.14*	.15*	.03	.31**	.28**	.45**	.24**	.07	1.00

* $p < .05$. ** $p < .001$.

coefficient of .51 exists between the variables streetwise and pre-prison criminality.

To further test for multicollinearity analysis of variance inflation factor (VIF) was performed. The largest VIF value among all independent variables is often used as an indicator of the severity of multicollinearity (Neter, Kutner, Nachtsheim, & Wasserman, 1996). A maximum VIF value in excess of 10 is frequently taken as an indication that multicollinearity may be unduly influencing the least squares estimates. VIF analysis of independent variables used in this study indicate that the highest VIF value is 1.272, well within acceptable limits.

In addition to VIF analysis, the condition index values were also used as a measure of multicollinearity . Belsley, Kuh, and Welsch (1980) propose that a condition index for a given model of 30 to 100 indicates moderate to severe multicollinearity . None of the models used in the present study reach the threshold of 30 or above. Therefore, based on the performed tests, multicollinearity is not problematic in this analysis.

Hypotheses

Based upon the literature and theoretical tenets described, this study tests the following hypotheses:

1. As measures of the pre-prison variables scales increase (streetwise, pre-prison criminality, frequency in the system, and negative parenting – Appendix 1), the in-prison variables will increase (participation in the inmate economy, victimization, witness victimization, adherence to the convict code – Appendix 2).

2. As measures of the in-prison variables scales increase (Appendix 2), the likelihood of developing PTSS as result of the prison experience increases (Appendix 3).
3. As measures of the pre-prison variables scales increase (streetwise, pre-prison criminality, frequency in the system, and negative parenting – Appendix 1), the likelihood of developing PTSS will increase (Appendix 3).

Analysis of the relationship between a combination of the pre-prison and in-prison independent variables implemented in this study, and development of PTSS is provided. This analysis further enlightens the analysis of between experiences and development of PTSS.

Regression Analysis

Regression analysis was performed to test the relationships between the pre-prison measures and the in-prison measures, between the in-prison measures and PTSS, and between the fully recursive model which measures effects of pre-prison and in-prison variables on PTSS. Unlike zero-order correlation that tests the significance, direction, and strength of association of bivariate relationships between variables, multiple regression examines the model and measures the significance, strength, and direction of association between each independent and dependent variable while holding all other independent variables constant. In addition, regression analysis, by standardizing the betas, allows the researcher to determine which independent variables have greater predictive power for likelihood of the dependent variable. Standardized betas (β) are reported in each regression table.

Table 4.2
Hypothesis 1 Regression Analysis:
Pre-Prison on In-Prison Variables

	Inmate Economy (Adj. R^2 = .33)	Victim (Adj. R^2 = .15)	Witness Victim (Adj. R^2 = .36)	Convict Code (Adj. R^2 = .31)
	β (SE)	β (SE)	β (SE)	β (SE)
Race	.005 (.258)	.178* (.280)	.015 (.369)	.189 (.137)
Education	.022 (.137)	−.022 (.148)	−.019 (.197)	.196 (.135)
Age First Prison	−.104 (.091)	−.049 (.098)	−.229** (.130)	−.181* (.089)
Pre-Prison Streetwise	.013 (.080)	.028 (.086)	.164* (.114)	.481** (.079)
Pre-Prison Criminality	.491** (.045)	.216* (.048)	.357** (.064)	.060 (.043)
Frequency in System	.044 (.076)	−.112 (.082)	−.020 (.109)	.009 (.074)
Negative Parenting	.138* (.022)	.294** (.024)	.096 (.032)	−.030 (.022)

* $p < .05$. ** $p < .001$, two-tailed.

Hypothesis 1: Findings

Hypothesis 1 predicts how the pre-prison variables will affect individual's adjustment to the prison environment. It is generally hypothesized that as measures of pre-prison variables increase, the in-prison measures will increase.

Model 1: Effects of Pre-Prison Variables on Inmate Economy (Adj. R^2 = .34)

Proposition 1.1a of hypothesis 1 states that as measures of streetwise increase, likelihood of participation in the inmate economy will increase. Correlation analysis indicates significant positive association between the streetwise measure and the in-prison measure of inmate economy (.32**). However, regression analysis does not indicate a significant relationship between streetwise and participation in the inmate economy (β = .013, SE = .080). Therefore model one does not support the proposition that streetwise increases the likelihood of participation in the inmate economy.

Proposition 1.1b of hypothesis 1 states that as measures of pre-prison criminality increase, the likelihood of participation in the inmate economy will increase. Correlation analysis indicates a positive association between pre-prison criminality and participation in the inmate economy (.57**). Also, regression analysis supports the proposition that pre-prison criminality will increase the likelihood of participation in the inmate economy (β = .491**, SE = .045). Therefore model 1 supports the proposition that increases in the pre-prison criminality measures increase the likelihood of participation in the inmate economy.

Proposition 1.1c of hypothesis 1 states that as measures of frequency in the system increase, likelihood of participation in the inmate economy will increase. Correlation analysis indicates a positive association between frequency in the system and participation in the inmate economy (.20**), however the correlation coefficient is less than .25. Regression analysis does not indicate a significant relationship between frequency in the system and participation in the inmate economy ($\beta = .044$, $SE = .076$). Therefore model 1 does not support the proposition that frequency in the system will increase the likelihood of participation in the inmate economy.

Proposition 1.1d of hypothesis 1 states that as measures of negative parenting increase, likelihood of participation in the inmate economy will increase. Correlation analysis indicates a positive association between negative parenting and participation in the inmate economy (.22**), however the correlation coefficient is less than .25. Regression analysis indicates a significant relationship between negative parenting and participation in the inmate economy ($\beta = .138*$, $SE = .022$). Therefore, model 1 supports the proposition that as measures of negative parenting increase the likelihood of participation in the inmate economy increases.

Hypothesis 1: Findings

Model 2: Effects of Pre-Prison Variables on In-Prison Victimization (Adj. R^2 = .15)

Proposition 1.2a of hypothesis 1 states that as measures of streetwise increase, likelihood of in-prison victimization will increase. Correlation analysis does not indicate a positive association between the control variable race and in-prison victimization, however, regression analysis does indicate a significant relationship between race and in-prison victimization (β = .178*, SE = .280). Correlation analysis indicates positive association between the streetwise measures and the in-prison measures of victimization (.15*), however the correlation coefficient is less than .25. Regression analysis does not indicate a significant relationship between streetwise and victimization (β = .028, SE = .086). Therefore, model one does not support the proposition that streetwise increase the likelihood of being victimized while in prison.

Proposition 1.2b of hypothesis 1 states that as measures of pre-prison criminality increase, the likelihood of in-prison victimization will increases. Correlation analysis indicates a positive association between pre-prison criminality and in-prison victimization (.25**). Also, regression analysis supports the proposition that pre-prison criminality will increase the likelihood of being victimized while incarcerated (β = .216*, SE = .048). Therefore, model 1 supports the proposition that negative parenting increases the likelihood of in-prison victimization.

Proposition 1.2c of hypothesis 1 states that as measures of frequency in the system increases, likelihood of in-prison victimization will increase. Correlation analysis does not indicate a positive association between frequency in the system and in-prison victimization. Regression analysis does not indicate a significant relationship between frequency in the system and in-prison victimization ($\beta = -.112$, $SE = .082$). Therefore model one does not support the proposition that frequency in the system will increase the likelihood of in-prison victimization.

Proposition 1.2d of hypothesis 1 states that as measures of negative parenting increases, likelihood of in-prison victimization will increase. Correlation analysis indicates a positive association between negative parenting and in-prison victimization (.32**). Further, regression analysis indicates a significant relationship between negative parenting and in-prison victimization ($\beta = .294**$, $SE = .024$). Therefore, model one supports the proposition that as measures of negative parenting increase the likelihood of being victimized while incarcerated increase.

Model 3: Effects of Pre-Prison Variables on Witnessing Victimization in Prison (Adj. R^2 = .36)

Proposition 1.3a of hypothesis 1 states that as measures of streetwise increase, likelihood of witnessing victimization in prison will increase. Correlation analysis indicates a significant negative association between the control variable age first prison and witnessing victimization (−.43**) and regression analysis indicates a significant relationship between age first prison and witnessing victimization in prison ($\beta = -.229**$, $SE = .130$). Correlation analysis indicates significant positive

Hypothesis 1: Findings

association between the streetwise measures and the in-prison measures of witnessing victimization (.44**). Further, regression analysis indicates a significant relationship between streetwise and witnessing victimization ($\beta = .164*$, $SE = .114$). Therefore model one supports the proposition that streetwise increase the likelihood of witnessing victimization while in prison.

Proposition 1.3b of hypothesis 1 states that as measures of pre-prison criminality increase, the likelihood of witnessing victimization in prison will increase. Correlation analysis indicates a positive association between pre-prison criminality and witnessing victimization (.55**). Also, regression analysis supports the proposition that pre-prison criminality will increase the likelihood of witnessing victimized while incarcerated ($\beta = .325**$, $SE = .064$). Therefore, model one supports the proposition that pre-prison criminality increases the likelihood of witnessing victimization while incarcerated.

Proposition 1.3c of hypothesis 1 states that as measures of frequency in the system increase, likelihood of witnessing victimization will increase. Correlation analysis indicates a positive association between frequency in the system and witnessing victimization (.17*), however the correlation coefficient is less than .25. Regression analysis does not indicate a significant relationship between frequency in the system and witnessing victimization ($\beta = -.020$, $SE = .109$). Therefore model one does not support the proposition that frequency in the system will increase the likelihood of witnessing victimization while incarcerated.

Proposition 1.3d of hypothesis 1 states that as measures of negative parenting increase, likelihood of witnessing victimization will increase. Correlation analysis indicates a positive association between negative parenting and in-prison victimization (.19**), however the correlation coefficient is less than .25. Regression analysis does not indicate a significant relationship between negative parenting and witnessing victimization ($\beta = .096$, $SE = .032$). Therefore, model one does not support the proposition that as measures of negative parenting increase the likelihood of witnessing victimization while incarcerated increase.

Model 4: Effects of Pre-Prison Variables on Adherence to the Convict Code (Adj. R^2 = .31)

Proposition 1.4a of hypothesis 1 states that as measures of streetwise increase, likelihood of adherence to the convict code will increase. Correlation analysis indicates a significant negative relationship between age first prison and adherence to the convict code (–.32**) and regression analysis indicates a significant relationship between age first prison and adherence to the convict code ($\beta = -.181*$, $SE = .089$). Correlation analysis indicates significant positive association between the streetwise measures and adherence to the convict code (.53**). Further, regression analysis indicates a significant relationship between streetwise and adherence to the convict code ($\beta = .481**$, $SE = .079$). Therefore, model 1 supports the proposition that streetwise increase the likelihood of adherence to the convict code.

Hypothesis 1: Findings

Proposition 1.4b of hypothesis 1 states that as measures of pre-prison criminality increase, the likelihood of adherence to the convict code will increase. Correlation analysis indicates a positive association between pre-prison criminality and adherence to the convict code (.37**). However, regression analysis does not support the proposition that pre-prison criminality will increase the likelihood of adherence to the convict code ($\beta = .060$, $SE = .043$). Therefore model 1 does not support the proposition that pre-prison criminality increase the likelihood of adherence to the convict code.

Proposition 1.4c of hypothesis 1 states that as measures of frequency in the system increases, likelihood of adherence to the convict code will increase. Correlation analysis indicates a positive association between frequency in the system and adherence to the convict code (.20**), however the correlation coefficient is less than .25. Regression analysis does not indicate a significant relationship between frequency in the system and adherence to the convict code ($\beta = .009$, $SE = .074$). Therefore model one does not support the proposition that frequency in the system will increase the likelihood of adherence to the convict code.

Proposition 1.4d of hypothesis 1 states that as measures of negative parenting increases, likelihood of adherence to the convict code will increase. Correlation analysis does not indicate a positive association between negative parenting and adherence to the convict code. Regression analysis does not indicate a significant relationship between negative parenting and adherence to the convict code ($\beta = .007$, $SE = .022$). Therefore, model one does not support the proposition that as measures of negative parenting increase the likelihood of witnessing victimization while incarcerated increases.

Table 4.3
Hypothesis 2 Regression Analysis: In-Prison on PTSS

	PTSS (Adj. R^2 = .29)
	β (*SE*)
Race	−.008 (.330)
Education	−.001 (.173)
Age First Prison	.090 (.117)
Inmate Economy	.185* (.086)
Victimization	.405** (.088)
Witness Victimization	.049 (.066)
Convict Code	−.034 (.087)

* $p < .05$. ** $p < .001$.

Hypothesis 2: Findings

Hypothesis 2 states that in-prison variables will affect onset of PTSS. Hypothesis 2 predicts that as measures of the in-prison variables increase, the likelihood of developing PTSS as result of the prison experience will increase.

Model 5: Effects of In-Prison Variables on Development of PTSS (Adj. R^2 = .22)

Proposition 1 of hypothesis 2 states that as the measures of participation in the inmate economy increase, the likelihood of developing PTSS as result of incarceration will increase. Correlation analysis indicates a positive association between participation in the inmate economy and developing PTSS as result of the prison experience (.29**). Regression analysis indicates a significant relationship between participation in the inmate economy and PTSS (β = .185*, SE = .086,). Therefore, findings support the proposition that stress induced by involvement in the inmate economy may cause PTSS.

Proposition 2 of hypothesis 2 states that as the measures of in-prison victimization increase, the likelihood of developing PTSS as result of incarceration will increase. Correlation analysis indicates a significant positive association between in-prison victimization and developing PTSS as result of the prison experience (.45**). Regression analysis indicates a significant relationship between in-prison victimization and PTSS (β = .405**, SE = .088). Therefore, findings support the proposition that in-prison victimization may result in onset of PTSS for some.

Proposition 3 of hypothesis 2 states that as the measures of witnessing victimization in prison increase, the likelihood of developing PTSS as result of the prison experience increases. Correlation analysis indicates a positive association between witnessing victimization and onset of PTSS as result of the prison experience (.24**). However, regression analysis does not indicate a significant relationship between witnessing victimization and onset of PTSS as result of the prison experience (β = .049, SE = .066). Therefore, the proposition that witnessing victimization in prison will increase the likelihood of developing PTSS is not supported.

Proposition 4 of hypothesis 2 states that adherence to the convict code increases likelihood of developing PTSS as result of the prison experience. Correlation analysis does not indicate a significant association between adherence to the convict code and development of PTSS as result of the prison experience. Regress analysis does not indicate a significant relationship between adherence to the convict code and development of PTSS as result of the prison experience (β = −.034, SE = .087). Therefore, the proposition that adherence to the convict code increases the likelihood of developing PTSS as result of the prison experience is not supported.

Table 4.4
ypothesis 3 Regression Analysis: Pre-Prison on PTSS

	PTSS (Adj. R^2 = .22)
	β (*SE*)
Race	.056 (.352)
Education	−.002 (.187)
Age First Prison	.035 (.124)
Pre-Prison Streetwise	.090 (.109)
Pre-Prison Criminality	.098 (.061)
Frequency in System	−.098 (.104)
Negative Parenting	.319**(.030)

* $p < .05$. ** $p < .001$.

Hypothesis 3: Findings

Hypothesis 3 predicts that as measures of streetwise, pre-prison criminality, frequency in the system, and measures of negative parenting increase, the likelihood of developing PTSS independent of the prison experience will increase.

Model 6: Effects of Pre-Prison Variables on Developing PTSS Independent of the Prison Experience (Adj. R^2 = .22)

Proposition 1 of hypothesis 3 states that as measures of streetwise increase, the likelihood of developing PTSS independent of the prison experience will increase. Correlation analysis indicates a positive relationship between streetwise and onset of PTSS independent of the prison experience (.14*), however the correlation coefficient is less than .25. Regression analysis does not indicate a significant relationship between streetwise and development of PTSS independent of the prison experience ($\beta = .090$, $SE = .109$). Therefore, model four does not support the proposition that a significant relationship exists between streetwise and development of PTSS independent of the prison experience.

Proposition 2 of hypothesis 3 states that as measures of pre-prison criminality increase, the likelihood of developing PTSS independent of the prison experience increases. Correlation analysis indicates a positive relationship between pre-prison criminality and development of PTSS independent of the prison experience (.15*), however the correlation coefficient is less than .25. Regression analysis does not indicate a significant relationship between pre-prison criminality and development of PTSS independent of the prison experience ($\beta = .098$, $SE = .061$). Therefore, model five does not support the proposition that a significant relationship exists between pre-prison criminality and development of PTSS independent of the prison experience.

Proposition 3 of hypothesis 2 states that as measures of frequency in the system increases, the likelihood of developing PTSS independent of the prison experience increases. Correlation analysis does not indicate a significant positive relationship between frequency in the system and developing PTSS independent of the prison experience. Regression analysis does not indicate a significant relationship between frequency in the system and development of PTSS independent of the prison

Hypothesis 3: Findings

experience (β = −.098, *SE* = .104). Therefore, model 6 does not support the proposition that a significant positive relationship exists between frequency in the system and development of PTSS independent of the prison experience.

Proposition 4 of hypothesis 3 states that as measures of pre-prison negative parenting increase, the likelihood of developing PTSS independent of the prison experience increases. Correlation analysis indicates a positive relationship between negative parenting and development of PTSS independent of the prison experience (.31**). Regression analysis indicates a significant relationship between negative parenting and development of PTSS independent of the prison experience (β = .319**, *SE* = .030). Therefore, model 6 supports the proposition that increased levels of negative parenting affect the development of PTSS independent of the prison experience.

Analysis of the Relationship Between a Combined Set of Pre-Prison and In-Prison Independent Variables With Development of PTSS

To gain further insight into stressors that may lead to the development of PTSS, analysis of the relationship between pre-prison and in-prison independent variables implemented in this study and the development of PTSS, is provided. This analysis further enlightens the analysis of potential stressors that may result in PTSS.

Table 4.5 Regression Analysis Fully Recursive Model: Pre-Prison and In-Prison Independent Variables and PTSS

	Dependent Variable
	PTSS (Adj. R^2 = .33)
Control Variables	β *(SE)*
Race	−.014(.336)
Education	.008 (.172)
Age First Prison	.075 (.118)
Pre-Prison Independent Variables	β *(SE)*
Pre-Prison Streetwise	.083 (.109)
Pre-Prison Criminality	.094 (.064)
Frequency in System	−.070(.096)
Negative Parenting	.180* (.030)
In-Prison Independent Variables	β *(SE)*
Inmate Economy	.101*(.094)
Victimization	.376**(.090)
Witness Victimization	.043 (.068)
Convict Code	−.017 (.094)

Model 7: Effect of Combined Set of Pre-Prison and In-Prison Independent Variables on Developing PTSS Independent of the Prison Experience (Adj. R^2 = .33)

Regression analysis of the combined set of in-prison independent variables and pre-prison independent variables reveals a significant relationship between the following independent variables with onset of PTSS: (a) pre-prison negative parenting (β = .180*, SE = .030), (b) in-prison participation in the inmate economy (β = .101*, SE = .094), and (c) in-prison victimization (β = .376**, SE = .090. The standardized beta for the relationship between in-prison victimization (.376**) and development of PTSS as result of the prison experience indicates stronger predictive power than that of negative parenting (β = .180*) or participation in the inmate economy (β = .101*).

Chapter 5. Summary, Discussion, Conclusion

Chapter 5. Summary, Discussion, Conclusion

Following is a summary of research objectives, hypotheses, and findings of the present study. The discussion section explains the significance of the findings and their relevance to previous research. Also considered are study limitations. The conclusion section addresses implications of study results, and recommendations for future research.

Research Objective

The general research objective was to test the effects of pre-prison variables on prison adjustment, of incarceration on the development of PTSS, and the potential of pre-prison experiences to result in PTSS independent of the prison experience. Also, to gain further understanding between traumatic events and development of PTSS analysis of the combined pre-prison and in-prison independent variables was performed.

The specific research questions, which guided the development and testing of the research hypotheses, were as follows:
1. What is the relationship between pre-incarceration attitudes and experiences, and characteristics of the incarceration experience?
2. What is the relationship between characteristics of the incarceration experience and developing PTSS?
3. What is relationship between characteristics of the pre-incarceration experience and onset of PTSS independent of the prison experience?
4. What is the relationship between a combination of the pre-prison and in-prison independent variables and development of PTSS?

Summary of Findings

Pre-Prison Variables on Prison Adjustment: Direct and/or Indirect Effects

Hypothesis 1 predicts how the pre-prison variables will affect individual's adjustment to the prison environment. It is generally hypothesized that as measures of pre-prison variables increase, the in-prison measures will increase.

The proposition that a significant relationship exists between pre-prison criminality and participation in the inmate economy is supported. This finding represents a direct effect between pre-prison experiences as preparation for in-prison activities. Involvement in criminality prior to incarceration prepares an individual to become involved in the "illegal" activities associated with the inmate economy: stealing merchandise to sell, collecting unpaid debts by use of force, extorting high interest on goods loaned, etc. This finding supports the tenets of the importation model espoused by Irwin and Cressey (1962).

The proposition that a significant relationship exists between negative parenting and participation in the inmate economy is supported. This finding represents an indirect effect between pre-prison experiences and in-prison activities. Scholars have found low socioeconomic status, unemployment, and being young parents to be related to negative parenting practices. Negative parenting has been found to be related to negative behavioral problems in children (Patterson, 1982; Wilson & Hernstein, 1985; Hagan & Palloni, 1990; Perry et al., 1992; Straus, 1994). Family stress associated with negative parenting leads to increased hostile interactions between parents and their children. This stress is fostered by inconsistent and harsh parenting practices. These types of negative interactions between parent and child may serve to instill anti-social tendencies, deteriorate the bond between parent and child, and increase the likelihood of the child becoming involved in delinquency and crime. The involvement in criminal activity, as result of negative parenting prior to incarceration, may indirectly prepare an individual for participation in the inmate economy.

The proposition that a significant relationship exists between pre-prison criminality and in-prison victimization is supported. This finding suggests a direct effect.

Involvement in criminality whether pre-prison or in-prison increases the likelihood of victimization (Cohen & Felson, 1979). The importation model (Irwin & Cressey, 1962) suggests that criminal tendencies pre-prison will be brought by the individual into the prison environment. Therefore, the likelihood of victimization in-prison is directly related to increased likelihood of victimization pre-prison. Wooldredge (1994) suggests that involvement in certain activities in the prison environment will increase the likelihood of victimization. He suggests that lack of participation in programs, participation in unsupervised activities, participation in rule breaking, etc. lead to increased victimization. These same elements apply to pre-prison activities and victimization (Hindelang, Gottfredson, & Garafolo, 1978).

The proposition that a significant relationship exists between negative parenting and in-prison victimization is supported. As described in the discussion of the indirect relationship between negative parenting and involvement in the inmate economy, a similar indirect relationship exists between negative parenting and in-prison victimization. Coercive strategies associated with negative parenting are counterproductive in developing "social competence" among youth (Hoffman, 1980; Peterson et al., 1985). Failed social bonding (Hirschi, 1969) as a result of negative parenting lead youth to disassociate from conventional norms and values. Gottfredson and Hirschi (1990) suggest that if social bonding does not occur by age 8, the result will be low levels of self-control, which in turn will lead to crime and analogous behaviors. Involvement in crime and analogous behaviors results in increased likelihood of victimization. Additionally, lack of self-control in the prison setting may also lead to increased victimization.

The proposition that streetwise and adherence to the convict code is supported. Streetwise (the "code of the street"; Anderson, 1999) and the convict code share common features. Both are belief systems comprised of specific rules, norms, and values. Inculcation into being streetwise forms a direct effect of preparation for adherence to the convict code.

In-Prison Variables on PTSS: Direct and/or Indirect Effects

Hypothesis 2 predicts how the in-prison variables will affect individual's likelihood of developing PTSS as result of the prison experience. It is generally hypothesized that as measures of in-prison variables increase, PTSS measures will increase.

The proposition that a significant relationship exists between participation in the inmate economy and development of PTSS is supported. The proposition that a significant relationship exists between in-prison victimization and development of PTSS is supported. These findings support the hypothesis that in-prison experiences affect development of PTSS as result of the incarceration experience.

The relationship between participation in the inmate economy and PTSS represents both direct and indirect effects. The significant finding of the association and relationship between participation in the inmate economy and onset of PTSS offers new information. A direct effect of participation in the inmate economy with onset of PTSS is that the stress associated with selling contraband within the strictures of the prison environment produces stress that reaches the level required to trigger PTSS. Therefore, this finding suggests that it is participation in the inmate economy independent of other factors that leads to onset of PTSS as result of the prison experience. An indirect effect between participation in the inmate economy and onset of PTSS is resultant victimization for failure to repay a debt. The convict code requires swift and strong recompense (victimization) for failure to repay. The literature is replete with studies that demonstrate the nexus between victimization and PTSS (Morgan et al., 2001; Foa et al., 1995; Kizer, 1996; Lorenz et al., 1993; Schwarz & Kowalski, 1991; Figley, 1978; Port et al., 2001; Solomon, 2001; Breslau et al., 1995).

The indirect effect of victimization associated with participation in the inmate economy may lead to PTSS for some. This is consistent with previous findings by Baker and Alfonse (2002), who reported that PTSD has been found among male and female incarcerated populations, and that the prevalence rate for PTSD is higher in the prison population than compared to the general population (Powell et al., 1997; Goff et al., 2007). Specifically, regression analysis performed in the present study demonstrates that elements of the incarceration experience, including participation in the inmate economy and in-prison victimization, are significantly related to development of PTSS as result of the prison experience.

The findings of this study are consistent with post-traumatic stress literature, which notes that victimization may be a source of PTSS (APA, 1994). Findings are also consistent with research assessing the incarceration experience. Findings indicate that prisoners experience victimization in prison. For example, Wooldredge (1998) stated that inmate crime is a serious type of inmate victimization, with theft being more common than assault.

Pre-Prison Variables on PTSS: Direct and/or Indirect Effects

Hypothesis 3 predicts how the pre-prison variables will affect individual's likelihood of developing PTSS independent of the prison experience. It is generally hypothesized that as measures of pre-prison variables increase, PTSS measures will increase.

The significant findings of the association and relationship between negative parenting and onset of PTSS support the hypothesis that PTSS may develop independent of the incarceration experience. As hypothesized, regression analysis indicates that pre-prison negative parenting is significantly related to onset of PTSS independent of the prison experience.

The relationship between negative parenting and onset of PTSS suggests both direct and indirect effects. Child neglect and abuse are forms of victimization that may directly result in PTSS. However, an indirect effect of negative parenting may also result in onset of PTSS. If a child is exposed to negative parenting this may lead to weakening of social bonds, failure to develop self-control, and externalization of antisocial tendencies. This process may lead to involvement in crime, delinquency, and analogous behaviors that will increase the child's likelihood of victimization. Increased victimization has been shown to result in PTSS.

These findings are consistent with the findings of previous research that demonstrates that pre-prison parental influences (Jang & Smith, 1997) and a variety of experiences associated with negative parenting (Chambers et al., 2000; Dembo et al., 1990; APA, 1994) may result in PTSS. However, as hypothesized for this study, regression analysis did not find pre-prison criminality nor attitudes to be significantly related to onset of PTSS independent of the prison experience. It may be that streetwise and actions actually insulate some individuals from developing PTSS.

Combined Pre-Prison and In-Prison Independent Variables on Development of PTSS: Direct and/or Indirect Effects

To gain further insight into the development of PTSS the relationship between the pre-prison and in-prison independent variables with development of PTSS was analyzed. In the analysis of the combined set of independent variables a significant relationship between negative parenting and development of PTSS was revealed. A significant relationship between in-prison participation in the inmate economy as well as victimization and development of PTSS were also revealed. These findings are consistent with the findings revealed in the pre-prison independent variables with PTSS analysis, as well as with the in-prison independent variables with PTSS analysis.

Elements of the Hypotheses Not Supported

The present study hypothesized that as the level of the streetwise measure, pre-prison criminality measure, frequency in the system measure, and negative parenting measure increased, the likelihood of the all of the in-prison measures would increase (participation in the inmate economy, in-prison victimization, witnessing victimization, and adherence to the convict code). The hypotheses assessed in this study were based on findings of previous research. However, several of the propositions contained in the hypotheses assessed were not supported.

The assumption of hypothesis 1 states that regression analysis would indicate significant relationships between each of the pre-prison variables and each of the in-prison variables. The propositions contained in hypothesis 1 are based upon the theoretical tenets and research findings contained in the literature review section of this study.

There are several potential explanations as to why each of the propositions contained in hypothesis 1 were not borne out. Data analyzed in this study were collected from a Midwestern state. The sample composition of this study may be dissimilar to the composition of samples from which previous findings were derived. It may be that the racial composition, educational levels, age first incarcerated, social interactions that govern attitudes, action patterns, and styles of parenting are dissimilar in the state from which the data were collected compared to other data bases. It may be that the prison environment itself determines participation in the inmate economy, likelihood of victimization, likelihood of witnessing victimization, and adherence to the convict code regardless of pre-prison experiences. Additionally, approximately 170 of the 208 respondents served their sentences in low-level custody institutions. The sample does not capture elements of the prison experience that exist in upper security level institutions. These findings suggest that the described limitations in generalizability associated with the sample should be tested in future research.

Witnessing victimization and adherence to the convict code were not found to be significant in predicting onset of PTSS as a result of the prison experience. It may be, given the violent nature of the prison environment, individuals become accustomed to seeing others victimized and therefore the traumatic aspect of witnessing victimization diminishes. It may be that the individuals included in the sample of this study were not exposed to the same frequency or intensity of witnessing victimization as was experienced by respondents in other samples.

The pre-prison variables streetwise, pre-prison criminality, and frequency in the system were not found to be significant in predicting PTSS. It may be that the variables streetwise and pre-prison criminality used in this study did not capture element used in previous research to predict development of PTSS. It may be that the composition of the sample analyzed in this study differs in characteristics from samples used in previous research.

Limitations

Since this study utilized a convenience sample, the findings may not generalize to a different population. Possible limitations of this study are sample selection and geographic location. Extraneous variables such as test reactivity and accuracy of self-reporting might have been present and unaccounted for. The survey instrument failed to note additional incarceration experiences such as overcrowding and solitary confinement, which may also have contributed to PTSS. Although limitations may be present, findings of this study need to be considered for the understanding of incarceration and pre-incarceration variables that may be related to PTSS. These findings need to be considered for program development as well as future research.

Implications

Although the present study provides findings that were limited to the variables assessed, outcomes indicate that there is support for the hypotheses that pre-incarceration experiences may affect prison adjustment, and that the incarceration experience has the potential to result in PTSS. Also tested is the potential for pre-prison experiences to lead to PTSS. An implication associated with onset of PTSS prior to incarceration is that the incarceration experience may in fact exacerbate pre-existing PTSS.

Ex-prisoners who suffer PTSS may face serious challenges upon their return to the community. Those who are released from prison face segregation, stigmatization, wage inequality, and a lack of mobility (Western,

2002; Harrison & Schehr, 2004). The challenges of reintegration for those with PTSS may be even greater than for individuals who do not face the complications associated with PTSS. These complications may further relate to problems such as substance use, criminal behavior, and re-incarceration.

As Yehuda and McFarlane (1995) pointed out, it is important to understand post-traumatic stress, which represents a constellation of symptoms that require a process of reaction to trauma events that include biological, psychological, and phenomenological dimensions. The individual who is exposed to a trauma (such as the prison experience) is left hyper-responsive to a variety of stimuli, which may be expressed in multiple behaviors. Thus, it is important to understand that the prison environment may be the causal agent in the onset of PTSS, and that those suffering PTSS during their period of incarceration require access to programs designed to meet their specific needs.

Public support for devoting additional resources to treating the mentally ill and physically compromised sector of the prison population may come from the application of a public health model. As pointed out by Conklin et al. (1998), medical and correctional communities have only recently realized the extent to which mental illness, substance use disorders, chronic disease, and communicable diseases, such as HIV/AIDS and tuberculosis (TB), are concentrated in the correctional system.

A key point is that correctional institutions are reservoirs of physical and mental illness, which constantly spill back into the community. If these illnesses are to be treated properly, transmission interrupted, and the health of the public protected, then effective treatment and education must be provided within the correctional system and continued beyond release.

Recommendations for Future Research

The present study provides support for the hypothesis that the incarceration experience and pre-incarceration experiences are linked to post-incarceration PTSS. Therefore, further study of this relationship is indicated. Since this study was limited by the factors investigated, it is recommended that a future study utilize a more in-depth survey instrument as well as multiple instruments for a more thorough examination of all possible variables (pre-prison and incarceration) that may be associated with PTSS. For example, adverse psychological consequences have been found in individuals subjected to solitary confinement (Gavora & Alexander, 1996; Gendreau & Keyes, 2001). Prison overcrowding has also been shown to exacerbate the detrimental aspects of prison incarceration (Schmid & Jones, 1993). In fact, the character of the prison incarceration experience itself may be a strong predictor of recidivism (Petersilia, 1994). A future study will need to explore relationships between overcrowding and solitary confinement (noted in the literature) on PTSS outcomes.

Additional variables that may be related to victimization and onset of PTSS have been noted in the literature and require future study. McCorkle (1993a, 1993b) reported that fear of crime inside correctional facilities leads to fear of victimization and that higher levels of fear inside the prison are associated with young prisoners, those socially isolated, and those more likely to be a frequent target of victimization. Since greater psychological damage may be associated with higher fear levels, this variable needs to be investigated.

This study's findings were also limited by the operational definitions of the variables. Additional studies have noted multiple types of victimization that may be found in prison. For example, O'Donnell and Edgar (1998) found that: in younger prisoners verbal abuse and exclusion rates were over twice as high; verbal abuse was most common, followed by threats and assaults; cell theft was the only type of victimization that was more common in older prisoners and this was followed by threats and verbal abuse; and lowest rates for all were for exclusion and robbery. Thus, it is recommended that a future study explore the multiple types of victimization experienced in prison (in more detail) and their direct relationship with PTSS outcomes.

In addition to these examples, previous studies have found that there are personality and demographic variables that are associated with prisoner reactions to stress and trauma. Silverman and Vega (1990) found that inmates each had a set of personal characteristics that affected their relationships with others and their overall prison experience. For example, intensity of expressions of anger was related to age, gender, marital status, and education. It has also been shown that personal coping resources and cultural factors are factors in psychiatric distress (Wheaton, 1983). These variables need further exploration to provide a complete understanding of PTSS as result of the incarceration experience.

Another important factor, which was not investigated

by the present study, is the effect of prison exposure to disease on PTSS outcomes. Previous studies have pointed out that prison inmates are exposed to infections and chronic diseases such as hepatitis C and AIDS. It is also noted that patients with illnesses of this type typically demonstrate despair, anger, frustration, hopelessness, and suicidal ideation. Acute stress such as this can lead to the development of PTSD (Burke, 2001; Morgan et al., 2001). Further, it may be that the fear of being exposed to these life-threatening diseases may result in the onset of PTSS. It is therefore recommended that a future study investigate the effect of disease exposure and fear of disease exposure as they relate to onset of PTSS.

The use of multiple types of measurement instruments would also help eliminate study limitations such as inaccuracy of self-reporting. For example, expert use of diagnostic tests would provide additional types of data; whereas the present study implements a symptoms-based approach, incorporating a clinical diagnostic criteria for a subsample of the respondents may enhance overall findings.

Since this study was limited by the use of a convenience sample, it is recommended that a future study utilize a more nationally representative sample. A future study using randomization procedures would lead to results that could be more widely generalized.

A flaw of this study is that it is based on cross-sectional and retrospective data. The present study cannot determine how the stage of criminal justice processing shapes results (Hochstetler, Murphy and Simons a, 2004). It cannot be determined if events that occur in prison have any bearing on rehabilitation and future success. Future research should contact and follow inmates through various stages in their sentences to determine with greater precision the direction and result of the relationships examined. The present study is the first stage in such a longitudinal study.

In summary, previous literature has pointed out that minimizing the socially and psychologically damaging outcomes of the prison incarceration experience can lead to a reduction in post-incarceration recidivism (O'Brien, 2001). Therefore, it is important to utilize this study's findings that the incarceration experience is linked to the onset of PTSS. Prisoners need be treated for this disorder prior to or upon their release.

This study points out specific variables that are related to PTSS outcomes. The prison lifestyle may include these factors that contribute to onset of PTSS and may be linked to future criminal behavior. This understanding can help prison officials become aware of conditions that need to be monitored or changed. Since these changes may not always be feasible, it is necessary to assess prisoners for PTSS and provide treatment accordingly.

Social and Economic Costs of Incarceration

Post-Incarceration: An "Army" of Releasees

The magnitude of the prison industrial complex underscores the importance of the tenets of the present study. As a society, we must understand that approximately 97 percent of those sentenced to incarceration will return to the community. This portends serious issues and potentially negative consequences for society at large.

Predicated upon sentencing policy promulgated by the Sentencing Commission under authority of the United States Congress, the prison population has soared to heretofore unparalleled numbers. The vast majority of these people, many of whom who have been subjected to the potentially deleterious aspects of the prison experience, are released to free society after they serve their time. The ramifications and potential consequences society may incur as result of physical and mental health problems acquired in prison are issues that need be addressed.

The effects of releasing prisoners who have experienced emotional, psychological, and physical damage as a result of incarceration may pose serious consequences for society. The increasing size of the prisoner population, use of restrictive and punitive practices, reduction of opportunities, use of solitary confinement, and increased numbers of maximum-security prisons add to this growing problem. It was estimated that in 2005 887,000 prisoners would be returned to the community (BJS, 2002). In 2008, 548,575 prisoners were released from state and federal prisons (BJS, 2009a). It is predicted that this group will be part of a growing trend of released prisoners who suffer symptom severity, including PTSS. The negative effect of prison upon individuals who have spent decades confined poses grave consequences for American society (Gorski, 2003). Just as individuals import characteristics acquired prior to incarceration into the prison environment, individuals who have spent extended periods locked in prison will export to the community characteristics they developed while incarcerated.

In addition to financial and social concerns, people released from prison may return to society with physical and emotional problems that may have direct implications for the community at large. Contagious diseases contracted in prison, such as AIDS, TB, or hepatitis C, can be spread to the community by the released prisoner. Psychological disorders, which may include PTSS, may lead to further debilitation for the ex-prisoner as well as to concerns for the community.

Gorski (2003) explains that ex-prisoners face post-incarceration syndrome (PICS), relapse, and recidivism. Gorski describes PICS as a set of symptoms found in many incarcerated and recently released prisoners that result from being subjected to prolonged incarceration in punitive environments. Gorski argues that the incarceration experience and subsequent development of PICS may lead to lack of post-release opportunities including education, job training, or rehabilitation. Gorski suggests that the prison experience may cause physical and psychological damage and that the labeled ex-con is blocked from legitimate opportunity. Gorski states that it is the prison experience itself and associated negative consequences that cause recidivism.

Incarceration: Costs to the Tax Payer

Beyond the social costs, the economic impact of the prison industrial complex needs to be considered. The most tangible cost of the "imprisonment binge" (Austin &

Irwin, 2000) is the cost to taxpayers. Since the enactment of mandatory minimum sentencing for drug users, the Federal Bureau of Prisons budget has increased by 1,954 percent: the agency's budget has jumped from $220 million in 1986 to $6.0 billion in 2010 (Executive Office of the President, 2010). The U.S. Department of Justice reports that in fiscal year 1999, the United States incurred direct expenditures for federal, state, and local justice systems in the amount of $146.5 billion (BJS, 2001b). In 2005, total expenditures rose to $186 billion, and Americans can be expected to spend an additional 27.5 billion more on new prisons before 2012 (Pew Charitable Trusts, 2007). Based on BOJ reports, the cost per inmate in 1999 included: (a) corrections spending which totaled $26,134 per inmate, (b) corrections, judicial, and legal costs which totaled $43,279 per inmate, and (c) corrections, judicial, legal, and police costs which totaled $78,154 per inmate. Adding to rapidly rising expenditures is the unprecedented rate of prison construction (BJS, 2003b), at a construction cost of approximately $100,000 per cell (Sentencing Project, 2010). This data provides cause to pause and re-evaluate contemporary sentencing practices in the United States.

Appendix 1. Independent Variables for Hypothesis 1

Streetwise (Cronbach's alpha = .72)

Prior to my last sentence I had a reputation of being a tough guy. Reverse coded
    1 = strongly disagree 6.8%
    2 = disagree 41.7%
    3 = agree 36.1%
    4 = strongly agree 15.0%
    (M = 2.60; SD = .83)

Prior to my last sentence I considered myself to be "streetwise." Reverse coded
    1 = strongly disagree 2.4%
    2 = disagree 11.5%
    3 = agree 53.8%
    4 = strongly agree 31.3%
    (M = 3.12; SD = .71)

Appendix 1. Independent Variables for Hypothesis 1

Prior to my sentence I was accustomed to dealing with streetwise people. Reverse coded
- 1 = strongly disagree 4.4%
- 2 = disagree 10.7%
- 3 = agree 52.9%
- 4 = strongly agree 32.0%

(M = 3.13; SD = .77)

Pre-Prison Criminality (Cronbach's alpha = .74)

Prior to my last sentence I broke the law on a regular basis. Reverse coded
- 1 = strongly disagree 6.8%
- 2 = disagree 30.6%
- 3 = agree 43.3%
- 4 = strongly agree 18.8%

(M = 2.75; SD = .84)

Prior to age 18 I carried a weapon. Coded
- 1 = never 45.9%
- 2 = about 1-2 times 24.4%
- 3 = about once/month 4.9%
- 4 = about once/week 7.3%
- 5 = 2-3 times/week or more 17.6%

(M = 2.26; SD = 1.53)

Prior to 18 I got into physical fights. Coded
- 1 = never 8.7%
- 2 = about 1-2 times 41.7%
- 3 = about once/month 25.2%
- 4 = about once/week 15.5%
- 5 = 2-3 times/week or more 8.7%

(M = 2.74; SD = 1.11)

Appendix 1. Independent Variables for Hypothesis 1

Outside of prison I pulled a weapon on someone. Coded
    1 = never 40.7%
    2 = about 1-2 times 44.6%
    3 = about once/month 8.8%
    4 = about once/week 2.9%
    5 = 2-3 times/week or more 2.9%
(M = 1.83; SD = .92)

Frequency in the Criminal Justice System (Cronbach's alpha = .63)

How many times have you been arrested? Coded
    1 = 1 .... 4.4%
    2 = 2 .... 2.9%
    3 = 3-5 .... 22.8%
    4 = 6-10 .... 26.7%
    5 = 11 or more 43.2%
(M = 4.03 or approximately 7 arrests; SD = 1.11)

How many times have you been in prison? Coded
    1 = 1 .... 38.3%
    2 = 2 .... 26.7%
    3 = 3-5 .... 30.6%
    4 = 6-10 .... 3.4%
    5 = 11 or more 1.0%
(M = 2.02 or approximately two prison terms; SD = .96)

Appendix 1. Independent Variables for Hypothesis 1

Influence of Negative Parenting (Cronbach's alpha = .87):

In a typical month during grade school or junior high how often:

(1) were your parents angry with you? Coded
- 1 = always 2.9%
- 2 = almost always 12.5%
- 3 = fairly often 31.3%
- 4 = about half the time 14.9%
- 5 = not too often 19.7%
- 6 = almost never 8.3%
- 7 = never 9.7%

($M = 4.0$; $SD = 1.60$)

(2) did your parents criticize your ideas? Coded
- 1 = always 10.0%
- 2 = almost always 17.5%
- 3 = fairly often 29.1%
- 4 = about half the time 12.1%
- 5 = not too often 10.2%
- 6 = almost never 8.7%
- 7 = never 6.3%

($M = 3.34$; $SD = 1.74$)

Appendix 1. Independent Variables for Hypothesis 1

(3) did your parents shout or yell at you because they were mad at you? Coded

    1 = always 4.4%
    2 = almost always 12.6%
    3 = fairly often 32.0%
    4 = about half the time 13.6%
    5 = not too often 15.4%
    6 = almost never 10.2%
    7 = never 11.7%
    (M = 4.00; SD = 1.69)

(4) did your parents ignore you when you tried to talk with them? Coded

    1 = always 22.0%
    2 = almost always 23.4%
    3 = fairly often 25.9%
    4 = about half the time 7.3%
    5 = not too often 9.1%
    6 = almost never 6.8%
    7 = never 5.4%
    (M = 3.00; SD = 1.74)

(5) did your parents push, shove, or grab you? Coded

    1 = always 4.4%
    2 = almost always 2.9%
    3 = fairly often 8.7%
    4 = about half the time 6.3%
    5 = not too often 30.6%
    6 = almost never 21.4%
    7 = never 25.7%
    (M = 5.22; SD = 1.79)

Appendix 1. Independent Variables for Hypothesis 1

(6) did your parents insult or swear at you? Coded
- 1 = always 6.3%
- 2 = almost always 6.8%
- 3 = fairly often 11.2%
- 4 = about half the time 9.2%
- 5 = not too often 21.8%
- 6 = almost never 24.8%
- 7 = never 19.9%

(M = 4.87; SD = 1.79)

(7) did your parents hit with their fists or an object slap, or spank with a paddle, a belt, or something else? Coded
- 1 = always 11.2%
- 2 = almost always 11.7%
- 3 = fairly often 10.2%
- 4 = about half the time 15.5%
- 5 = not too often 20.4%
- 6 = almost never 15.5%
- 7 = never 15.5%

(M = 4.31; SD = 1.93)

Appendix 2. Operational Definitions of In-Prison Dependent Variables for Hypothesis 1 and Independent Variables for Hypothesis 2

Participation in the inmate economy
(Cronbach's alpha = .69)

While in prison ...

(1) how often did you loan out goods for a profit? Coded
    1 = never 32.5%
    2 = about 1-2 times 28.2%
    3 = about once/month 13.1%
    4 = about once/week 11.2%
    5 = 2-3 times per week or more ... 15.0%
(M = 2.48; SD = 1.43)

Appendix 2. Operational Definitions of In-Prison Dependent Variables

(2) did you pay other prisoners to do work for you? Coded

    1 = never 68.3%
    2 = about 1-2 times 18.5%
    3 = about once/month 6.3%
    4 = about once/week 4.9%
    5 = 2-3 times per week or more ... 2.0%
    ($M = 1.54$; $SD = .95$).

Victimization in Prison (Cronbach's alpha = .59)

While in prison, how often . . .

(1) was something of yours stolen or vandalized? Coded

    1 = never 40.3%
    2 = about 1-2 times 52.9%
    3 = about once/month 4.3%
    4 = about once/week 1.5%
    5 = 2-3 times per week or more ... 1.0%
    ($M = 1.70$; $SD = .71$)

(2) did another prisoner con you or scam you out of property or commissary? Coded

    1 = never 55.1%
    2 = about 1-2 times 38.0%
    3 = about once/month 4.9%
    4 = about once/week 2.0%
    5 = 2-3 times per week or more ... 0.0%
    ($M = 1.54$; $SD = .68$)

Appendix 2. Operational Definitions of In-Prison Dependent Variables

(3) did another prisoner take property from you using force or intimidation? Coded
    1 = never 90.3%
    2 = about 1-2 times 8.7%
    3 = about once/month 0.5%
    4 = about once/week 0.0%
    5 = 2-3 times per week or more ... 0.5%
    ($M = 1.12$; $SD = .41$)

(4) were you threatened with violence? Coded
    1 = never 40.0%
    2 = about 1-2 times 47.8%
    3 = about once/month 7.3%
    4 = about once/week 2.0%
    5 = 2-3 times per week or more ... 2.9%
    ($M = 1.8$; $SD = .88$)

(5) were you assaulted with a weapon? Coded
    1 = never 85.0%
    2 = about 1-2 times 14.4%
    3 = about once/month 0.5%
    4 = about once/week 0.0%
    5 = 2-3 times per week or more ... 0.0%
    ($M = 1.56$; $SD = .38$)

Appendix 2. Operational Definitions of In-Prison Dependent Variables

Witnessing Others Victimized (Cronbach's alpha = .83)

While in prison...

(1) I saw another prisoner seriously injured. Coded
    1 = never 24.3%
    2 = about 1-2 times 51.9%
    3 = about once/month 14.6%
    4 = about once/week 6.8%
    5 = 2-3 times per week or more ... 2.4%
    (M = 2.11; SD = .93)

(2) I saw another prisoner killed. Coded
    1 = never 91.7%
    2 = about 1-2 times 7.3%
    3 = about once/month 0.5%
    4 = about once/week 0.5%
    5 = 2-3 times per week or more ... 0.0%
    (M = 1.10; SD = .36)

(3) I witnessed another prisoner's property being stolen or vandalized. Coded
    1 = never 27.7%
    2 = about 1-2 times 41.7%
    3 = about once/month 16.0%
    4 = about once/week 11.7%
    5 = 2-3 times per week or more ... 2.9%
    (M = 2.20; SD = 1.06)

Appendix 2. Operational Definitions of In-Prison Dependent Variables

(4) I was aware of other prisoners' being raped. Coded
- 1 = never 57.8%
- 2 = about 1-2 times 34.5%
- 3 = about once/month 5.8%
- 4 = about once/week 0.5%
- 5 = 2-3 times per week or more ... 1.5%

($M = 1.53$; $SD = .76$)

(5) I witnessed other prisoners' being assaulted with a weapon. Coded
- 1 = never 43.7%
- 2 = about 1-2 times 46.1%
- 3 = about once/month 5.8%
- 4 = about once/week 2.9%
- 5 = 2-3 times per week or more ... 1.5%

($M = 1.72$; $SD = .82$)

(6) I witnessed physical fights. Coded
- 1 = never 7.8%
- 2 = about 1-2 times 38.8%
- 3 = about once/month 28.2%
- 4 = about once/week 16.0%
- 5 = 2-3 times per week or more ... 9.2%

($M = 2.80$; $SD = 1.09$)

Appendix 2. Operational Definitions of In-Prison Dependent Variables

Adherence to the convict code (Cronbach's alpha = .75)

While in prison...

(1) I was confident a friend or associate would watch my back. Reverse coded
  1 = strongly disagree 6.3%
  2 = disagree 15.6%
  3 = agree 49.8%
  4 = strongly agree 28.3%
  (M = 3.00; SD = .83)

(2) I regularly watched a friend's or associate's back. Reverse coded
  1 = strongly disagree 5.9%
  2 = disagree 19.0%
  3 = agree 47.8%
  4 = strongly agree 27.3%
  (M = 2.97; SD = .83

(3) I lived by the convict code. Reverse coded
  1 = strongly disagree 5.4%
  2 = disagree 15.2%
  3 = agree 53.9%
  4 = strongly agree 25.5%
  (M = 3.00; SD = .79)

Appendix 3. Post-Traumatic Stress Diagnostic Scale: UM-CIDI Dependent Variable for Hypothesis 2

Dependent Variable for Hypothesis 3
(Cronbach's alpha = .90)

(1) Did you keep remembering the event when you did not want to?
 No (58.3%); Yes (41.7%).

(2) Did you keep having dreams or nightmares about it?
 No (78.2%); Yes (21.8%).

(3) Did you ever suddenly act or feel that the event was happening again, when it was not?
 No (83.5%); Yes (16.5%).

(4) Did you ever get very upset when you were in a situation that reminded you of it?
 No (64.6%); Yes (35.4%).

Appendix 3. Post-Traumatic Stress Diagnostic Scale: UM-CIDI Dependent Variable

(5) After the experience, did you find that you no longer had loving or warm feelings toward anyone?
    No (84.9%); Yes (15.1%).

(6) Did you ever go out of your way to avoid situations that remind you of the event?
    No (61.7%); Yes (38.3%).

(7) Did you try hard not to think about it?
    No (60.7); Yes (39.3%).

(8) Did you develop a memory blank so that you could not remember certain things about the event?
    No (85.4%); Yes (14.6%).

(9) Did you feel isolated or distant from others after the event?
    No (72.2%); Yes (27.8%).

(10) Did you begin to feel that there was no point in thinking about the future?
    No (76.7%}; Yes (23.3%).

(11) Did you lose interest in doing things that used to be important to you?
    No (73.3); Yes (26.7%).

(12) Did you have more trouble concentrating than is usual for you?
    No (71.4%); Yes (28.6%).

(13) Did you act unusually irritable or lose your temper a lot?
    No (68.4%); Yes (31.6).

Appendix 3. Post-Traumatic Stress Diagnostic Scale: UM-CIDI Dependent Variable

(14) Did you have more trouble sleeping than is usual for you?
   No (66.5%); Yes (33.5%).

(15) Did you become overly concerned about danger or become overly careful?
   No (77.2%); Yes (22.8%).

(16) Did you become jumpy or easily startled by ordinary noises or movements?
   No (75.6%); Yes (24.4%).

(17) Did you sweat or did your heart beat fast or did you tremble or get nauseous when you thought about the upsetting experience?
   No (78.6%); Yes (21.4%).

Appendix 4. Operational Definitions of Pre-Prison Control Variables for Hypotheses 1 and 3

Race:
- (1) White 60.9%
- (2) Other 39.1%

Education:
- (1) grade school or less 1.5%
- (2) some high school 26.7%
- (3) completed high school 39.8%
- (4) completed high school plus other training 27.7%
- (5) completed college 3.9%
- (6) don't know 0.5%

Appendix 4. Operational Definitions of Pre-Prison Control Variables

Age First Arrested:
- (1) 05-10 .... 9.2%
- (2) 11-12 .... 13.5%
- (3) 13-14 .... 17.4%
- (4) 15-16 .... 16.4%
- (5) 17-18 .... 18.8%
- (6) 19-22 .... 11.1%
- (7) 23-25 .... 4.3%
- (8) 26-30 .... 3.9%
- (6) 31 or more 5.3%

Age First Prison Sentence:
- (1) 15-16 .... 1.9%
- (2) 17-18 .... 18.8%
- (3) 19-22 .... 34.8%
- (4) 23-25 .... 9.7%
- (5) 26-30 .... 13.0%
- (6) 31 or more 21.7%

References

Adams, K. (1992). Adjusting to prison life. In M. Tonry (Ed.), *Crime and justice*, pp. 275-359. Chicago: University of Chicago Press.

American Psychiatric Association. (1980). *Diagnostic and statistical manual of mental disorders* (3rd ed.). Washington, DC: Author.

American Psychiatric Association. (1987). *Diagnostic and statistical manual of mental disorders* (3rd ed., rev.). Washington, DC: Author.

American Psychiatric Association. (1994). *Diagnostic and statistical manual of mental disorders* (4th ed.). Washington, DC: Author.

American Psychiatric Association. (2000). *Diagnostic and statistical manual of mental disorders* (4th ed., text rev.). Washington, DC: Author.

Anderson, E. (1999). *Code of the street: Decency, violence, and moral life of the inner city*. New York: W. W. Norton.

Aneshensel, C. (1999). Surveying the field. In C. Aneshensel & C. Phalan, (Eds.), *Handbook of sociology mental health*. Dordrecht, Netherlands: Kluwer Academic Publishers.

Austin, J., & Irwin, J. (2000). It's about time: America's imprisonment binge. Belmont, CA: Wadsworth.

Bacon, M. H. (1985). *The quiet rebels: The story of the Quakers in America*. Philadelphia: New Society Publishers.

Baker, C., & Alfonso, C. (2002). PTSD and criminal behavior. A national center for PTSD fact sheet. National Center for PTSD, Department of Veterans Affairs. Retrieved from http://www.ptsd.va.gov

Bartollas, C. (1982). Survival problems of adolescent prisoners. In R. Johnson and H. Toch (Eds.), *The pains of imprisonment*. Beverly Hills, CA: Sage.

Beaton, A., Cook, M., Cavanaugh, K., & Herrington, C. (2000). The psychological impact of burglary. *Psychology, Crime and Law*, 6, 33-43.

Becker, H. (1963). *Outsiders: Studies in the sociology of deviance*. New York: Free Press.

Belsley, D., Kuh, E., & Welsch, R. (1980). *Regression diagnostics: Identifying influential data and sources of collinearity*. New York: Wiley.

References

Benotsch, E. G., Brailey, K., Vasterling, J. J., Udo, M., Constans, J. I., & Sutkers, P. B. (2000). War zone stress, personal and environmental resources, and PTSD symptoms in Gulf War veterans: A longitudinal perspective. *Journal of Abnormal Psychology, 109,* 205-213.

Bohrnstedt, G., & Knoke, D. (1994). *Statistics for social data analysis.* Ilasca, IL: Peacock.

Bonta, J., & Gendreau, P. (1990). Reexamining the cruel and unusual punishment of prison life. *Law and Human Behavior, 14,* 347-342.

Breslau, N., Davis, G. C., & Andreski, P. (1995). Risk factors for PTSD related traumatic events: A prospective analysis. *American Journal of Psychiatry, 152,* 529-535.

Brinded, P., Alexander, M. J., Simpson, I. P, Laidlaw, T. M., Parley, N., & Piona, M. (2001). Prevalence of psychiatric disorders in New Zealand prisons: A national study. *Australian and New Zealand Journal of Psychiatry, 35,* 166-173.

Bukstel, L. H., & Kilmann, P. R. (1980). Psychological effects of imprisonment on confined individuals. *Psychological Bulletin, 88,* 469-493.

Bureau of Justice Statistics. (1997). *Lifetime likelihood of going to state or federal prison.* Washington, DC: U.S. Department of Justice.

Bureau of Justice Statistics. (1997). *Mental health and treatment of inmates and probationers* (Report No. 174463). Washington, DC: U.S. Department of Justice.

Bureau of Justice Statistics. (2001a). *Federal criminal case processing, November 2000* (p. 12). Washington, DC: U.S. Department of Justice.

Bureau of Justice Statistics. (2001b). *Justice expenditures and employment extracts: 1992-1999.* Washington, DC: U.S. Department of Justice. Retrieved June 3, 2003, from http://www.ojp.usdoj.gov/bjs/eande/htm

Bureau of Justice Statistics. (2002). *Justice expenditure and employment in the US, 1999.* Washington DC: U.S. Department of Justice.

Bureau of Justice Statistics. (2003a). *Jail, prison, probation, and parole.* Washington, DC: U.S. Department of Justice. Retrieved June 23, 2003, from http://www.ojp.usdoj.gov/bjs/abstract/ppus02.htm

Bureau of Justice Statistics. (2003b). *Prevalence of imprisonment in the U.S. population, 1974-2001.* Washington, DC: U.S. Department of Justice.

Bureau of Justice Statistics. (2009a). *Prisoners in 2008.* Washington, DC: U.S. Department of Justice.

Bureau of Justice Statistics. (2009b). *Probation.* Washington, DC: U.S. Department of Justice.

Bureau of Justice Statistics. (2009). *Prisoners Released* (NCJ 228417, Dec. 2009). Retrieved June 20, 2011, from http://bjs.ojp.usdoj.gov/content/pub/pdf/p08.pdf

Burke, K. W. (2001). Psychiatric aspects of hepatitis C treatment in prison. *Corrections Today, 63*(5), 75-79.

Caballero, M. A., Ramos, L., & Saltijeral, M. T. (2000). Posttraumatic stress dysfunction and other reactions of the victims of house burglary. *Salud Mental, 23,* 8-17.

References

Chambers, J. A., Power, K. G., Loucks, N., & Swanson, V. (2000). The quality of perceived parenting and its association with peer relationships and psychological distress in a group of incarcerated young offenders. *International Journal of Offender Therapy and Comparative Criminology, 44*, 350-368.

Chiles, J. A., von Cleve, E., Jemelka, R. P., & Trupin, E. W. (1990). Substance abuse and psychiatric disorders in prison inmates. *Hospital and Community Psychiatry, 41*, 1132-1134.

Clemmer, D. (1940). *The prison community.* Boston: The Christopher Publishing House.

Cohen, L., & Felson, M. (1976). Prison violence: A sociological perspective. In A. K. Cohen, G. F. Cole, & R. G. Bailey (Eds.), *Prison violence* (pp. 3-22). Lexington, MA: Lexington Books.

Cohen, L., & Felson, M. (1979). Social change and crime rate trends: A routine activity approach. *American Sociological Review, 44*, 588-608.

Cohen, L., & Felson, M. (1997). A general theory of subcultures. In K. Gelder & S. Thorton (Eds.), *The subculture reader.* London: Routledge. (Original work published in 1955)

Conklin, T.J., Lincoln, T. & Flanigan, T.P. (1998). A public health model to connect correctional health care with communities. *American Journal of Public Health, 88*, 1249-1250.

Cooper, C., & Berwick, S. (2001). Factors affecting psychological well-being of three groups of suicide prone prisoners. *Current Psychology, 20*, 169-182.

Cooperstein, M. A. (2001). Corrections officers: The forgotten police force. *Pennsylvania Psychologist Quarterly, 61*(5), 7-23.

Davis, R. C., Taylor, B., & Lurigio, A. J. (1996). Adjusting to criminal victimization: The correlates of post crime distress. *Violence and Victims, 11*, 21-38.

Davison, S., Leese, M., & Taylor, P. (2001). Examination of the screening properties of the Personality Diagnostic Questionnaire 4+ (PDQ-4+) in a prison population. *Journal of Personality Disorders, 15*, 180-194.

Dembo, R., Williams, L., La Voie, L., Berry, E., Getreau, A., Kern, J., Genung, L., Schmeidler, J., Wish, E. D., & Mayo, J. (1990). Physical abuse, sexual victimization and marijuana/hashish and cocaine use over time: A structural analysis among a cohort of high risk youth. *Journal of Prison and Jail Health, 9*, 13-43.

Denkers, A. J. M., & Winkel, F. W. (1997). Crime victims' well-being and fear in a prospective and longitudinal study. *International Review of Victimology, 5*, 141-162.

Ditton, P. M. (1999). *Bureau of Justice Statistics Special Report: Mental health and treatment of inmates and probationers.* Washington, DC: U.S. Department of Justice. Retrieved August 7, 2003, from http://www.ojp.usdoj.gov

Dohrenwend, B. P. (2000). The role of adversity in psychopathology: Some evidence and its implications for theory and research. *Journal of Health and Social Behavior, 41*, 1-19.

Durkheim, E. (1982). *The rules of the sociological method* (W. E. Halls, Trans.). New York: Free Press. (Original work published 1895)

References

Eck, J. (1994). *Drug markets and drug places: A case-control study of the spatial structure of illicit drug dealing.* Unpublished doctoral dissertation, University of Maryland, College Park.

Eck, J., & Weisburd, D. (1995). *Crime and place.* Monsey, NY: Criminal Justice Press.

Elliott, D., Juizinga, D., & Ageton, S. (1985). *Explaining delinquency and drug use.* Beverly Hills, CA: Sage.

Elliot, D., Juizinga, D., & Menard, S. (1989). *Multiple problem youth: Delinquency, substance use, and mental health problems.* New York: Springer-Verlag.

Ex-Services Mental Welfare Society. (2003). Retrieved August 1, 2003, from http://www.combatstress.org.uk/news/current_issues.asp

Executive Office of the President. (2010). *Budget of the US Government 2010*, (p. 747). Washington, DC: U.S. Government Printing Office.

Federal Bureau of Prisons. (2010). *Weekly population report.* Retrieved July 1, 2010, from http://www.bop.gov

Figley, C. (1978). *Stress disorders among Vietnam veterans: Theory research and treatment implications.* New York: Bruner Mazel.

Florida Corrections Commission Annual Report. (1999). *Suicide in prison.* Retrieved June 22, 2003, from http://www.fcc.state.fl.us

Foa, E. B., Riggs, D. S., & Gershuny, B. S. (1995). Arousal, numbing, and intrusion: Symptom structure of PTSD following assault. *American Journal of Psychiatry, 152*(1), 116-122.

Fuller, D., & T. Orsagh. (1977). Violence and victimization within a state prison system. *Criminal Justice Review, 2*, 35-55.

Garofalo, J. (1987). Reassessing the lifestyle model of criminal victimization. In M. Gottfredson & T. Hirschi (Eds.), *Positive criminology.* Newbury Park, CA: Sage.

Gavora, J., & Alexander, E. (1996, 28 October). Is the Justice Department putting prisoners' rights ahead of citizens' security? *Insight on the News, 12*(40), 26-29.

Gendreau, P., & Keyes, D. (2001). Making prisons safer and more humane environments. *Canadian Journal of Criminology, 43*(1), 123-130.

Giddons, F. H. (1895). Is the term 'social class' a scientific category? *Proceedings of the National Conference of Charities and Correction, New Haven, CT,* 110-116.

Goff, A., Rose, E., Rose, S.., & Purves, D. (2007). Does PTSD occur in sentenced prison populations? *Criminal Behavior & Mental Health, 17*(3), 152-162.

Goffman, E. (1961). *Asylums: Issues on the social situation of mental patients and other inmates.* Garden City, NY: Anchor Books.

Goffman, E. (1963). *Stigma: Notes on spoiled identity.* Englewood Cliffs, NJ: Prentice Hall.

Gold, P. B., Engdahl, B. E., Eberly, R. E., Blake, R. J., Page, W. F., & Freuh, B. C. (2000). Trauma exposure, resilience, social support, and PTSD construct validity among former prisoners of war. *Social Psychiatry and Psychiatric Epidemiology, 35,* 36-42.

Goodstein, L. (1979). Inmate adjustment to prison and the transition to community life. *Journal of Research in Crime and Delinquency, 16,* 246-272.

References

Goodstein, L., MacKenzie, D., & Shortland, R. L. (1984). Personal control and inmate adjustment to prison. *Criminology, 22,* 343-369.

Gorski, T. T. (2003). Post-incarceration syndrome and relapse. Retrieved May, 25, 2003, from http://www.tgorski.com/criminal_justice/cjs_pics_&_relapse.htm

Gottfredson, M., & Hirschi, T. (1990). *A general theory of crime.* Stanford, CA: Stanford University Press.

Greenburg, G., & Rosencheck, R. (2009). Mental health and other risk factors for jail incarceration among male veterans. *Psychiatric Quarterly, 80,* 41-53.

Greene, S., Haney, C., & Hurtado, A. (2000). Cycles of pain: Risk factors in the lives of incarcerated mothers and their children. *The Prison Journal, 80*(1), 3-23.

Gujarati, D. (1988). *Basic economics.* New York: McGraw-Hill.

Gullone, E., Jones, T., & Cummins, R. (2000). Coping styles and prison experience as predictors of psychological well-being in male prisoners. *Psychiatry, Psychology and Law, 7,* 170-181.

Guthrie, R. K. (1999). *The prevalence of posttraumatic stress disorder among federal prison inmates.* Unpublished doctoral dissertation, West Virginia University.

Hagan, J. & Palloni, A. (1990). The social reproduction of a criminal class in working-class London, circa 1950-1980. *American Journal of Sociology, 96,* 265-299.

Haney, C. (1997). Psychology and the limits of prison pain: Confronting the coming crisis in Eighth Amendment law. *Psychology, Public Policy, and Law, 3,* (4), 499-588.

Haney, C. and P.G. Zimbardo (1998). The past and future of U.S. prison policy: Twenty-five years after the Stanford Prison Experiment. *American Psychologist, 53,* 709-727.

Harrison, B., & Schehr, R. C. (2004). Offenders and post-release jobs: Variables influencing success and failure. *Journal of Offender Rehabilitation, 39*(3), 35-68.

Haynes, F. E. (1948). The sociological study of the prison community. *Journal of Criminal Law and Criminology, 39,* 432-440.

Headland, T., Pike, K., & Harris, M. (1990). *Emics and etics: The insider/outsider debate.* Thousand Oaks, CA: Sage.

Hemmens, C. & Marquart, J.W. (1999). Straight time: Inmate's perceptions of violence and victimization in the prison environment. *Journal of Offender Rehabilitation, 28,* 1-21.

Hindelang, M., Gottfredson, M., & Garofalo, J. (1978). *Victims of personal crime: An empirical foundation for a theory of personal victimization.* Cambridge, MA: Ballinger.

Hirschi, T. (1969). *Causes of delinquency.* Berkeley, CA: University of California Press.

Hochstetler, A., Murphy, D. S., & Simons, R. L. (2004). Damaged goods: Exploring the predictors of distress in prison inmates. *Journal of Crime and Delinquency, 50*(3), 136-458.

Hodgins, S., & Cote, G. (1990). Prevalence of mental disorders among penitentiary inmates in Quebec. *Canada's Mental Health, 38,* 1-4.

Hoffman, M. L. (1980). Moral development in adolescence. In J. Adelson (Ed.), *Handbook of adolescent psychology.* New York: Wiley.

Horwitz, A., & Scheid, L. (1999). *A handbook for the study of mental health: Social contexts, theories, and systems.* New York: Cambridge University Press.

Hraba, J., Lorenz, F. O., Pechacova, Z., & Bao, W. D. (1999). Criminal victimization and distress in the Czech Republic. *Journal of Interpersonal Violence, 14,* 1030-1054.

Irwin, J. (1970). *The felon.* Englewood Cliffs, NJ: Prentice Hall.

Irwin, J. (1980). *Prisons in turmoil.* Boston: Little Brown.

Irwin, J., & Cressey, D. (1962). Thieves, convicts, and the inmate subculture. *Social Problems, 10,* 142-155.

Jaman, D. (1972). *A synopsis of research report no. 43.* Sacramento, CA: California Department of Corrections.

Jang, S. J., & Smith, C. A. (1997). A test of reciprocal causal relationships among parental supervision, affective ties, and delinquency. *Journal of Research in Crime and Delinquency, 34*(30), 1-31.

Johnson, R. (1976). *Culture and crisis in confinement.* Lexington, MA: Lexington.

Kessler, R. C., Sonnega, A., Bromet, E., Hughes, M., Nelson, C., & Breslau, N. (1999). Epidemiological risk factors for trauma and PTSD. In Rachel Yehuda (Ed.), *Risk factors for posttraumatic stress disorder* (pp. 1-22). Washington, DC: American Psychiatric Press.

Kessler, R.C. (1979). Stress, Social Status, and Psychological Distress. *Journal of Health and Social Behavior, 20,* 259-272.

Kizer, K. W. (1996). Progress on post-traumatic stress disorder. *Journal of the American Medical Association, 275,* 1149-1151.

Kopel, D. B. (1994). *Prison blues: How America's foolish sentencing policies endanger public safety* (Cato Policy Analysis No. 208). Washington, DC: Cato Institute. Retrieved September 5, 2003, from http://www.cato.org/pubs/pas/pa-208.html

Logan, T. K., Walker, R., Stanton, M., & Leukefeld, C. (2001). Substance use and intimate violence among incarcerated males. *Journal of Family Violence, 16,* 93-114.

Lombrosos, C., & Ferrero, W. (1895). *The female offender.* London: Unwin Fisher.

Lorenz, F. O., Conger, R. D., Montague, R. B., & Wickrama, K. A. S. (1993). Economic conditions, spouse support, and psychological distress of rural husbands and wives. *Rural Sociology, 58,* 247-268.

Lovell, D., Gagliardi, G. J., & Peterson, P. D. (2002). Recidivism and use of services among persons with mental illness after release from prison. *Psychiatric Services, 53* (10), 1290-1296.

Maitland, A. S., & Sluder, R. D. (1996). Victimization in prisons: A study of factors related to the general well-being of youthful inmates. *Federal Probation, 60*(2), 24-31.

McCaffrey, B. (U.S. General, retired). (1996). Keynote address: Opening plenary session, National Conference on Drug Abuse Prevention Research, National Institute on Drug Abuse. Retrieved May, 10, 2003, from http://www.165.112.78.61/MeetSum/CODA/Keynote2.html

McCorkle, R. C. (1992). Personal precautions to violence in prison. *Criminal Justice and Behavior, 19,* 160-173.

References

McCorkle, R. C. (1993a). Living on the edge: Fear in a maximum security prison. *Journal of Offender Rehabilitation, 20*, 73-91.

McCorkle, R. C. (1993b). Fear of victimization and symptoms of psychopathology among prison inmates. *Journal of Offender Rehabilitation, 19*, 27-41.

McFarlane, A. C. (1989). Victimization in prisons: A study of factors related to the general well-being of youthful inmates. *Federal Probation, 60*, 24-31.

Mead, G. H. (1934). *Mind, self, and society*. Chicago: University of Chicago Press.

Mirowsky, J., & Ross, C. E. (1999). Well-being across the life course. In A. V. Horwitz and T. L. Scheid (Eds.), *A handbook for the study of mental health: Social contexts, theories, and systems*, (pp. 328-347). New York: Cambridge University Press.

Morgan, C., Hazlett, G., Wang, S., & Richardson, E. G. (2001). Symptoms of dissociation in humans experiencing acute, uncontrollable stress: A prospective investigation. *American Journal of Psychiatry, 158*, 1239-1247.

Murphy, Daniel, S. (2007). An ex-convict teaches criminal justice: The etics-emics debate and the role of subjectivity in academia. *Justice Policy Journal, 4*(1), 1-21.

Murphy, Daniel S. (2003). The prison population binge. *The Blanket*. August 3, 2003. Archives available on line: http://indiamond6.ulib.iupui.edu:81/index.html

Myers, L., & Levy, G. (1978). Description and predictions of the intractable inmate. *Journal of Research in Crime and Delinquency, 15*, 214-228.

Neter, J., Kutner, M.H., Nachtsheim, C.J. & Wasserman, W. (1996). *Applied Linear Statistical Models (4th ed)*. Chicago: Irwin.

Norris, F. H., & Kaniasty, K. (1994). Psychological distress following criminal victimization in the general population. *Journal of Consulting and Clinical Psychology, 62*, 111-123.

O'Brien, P. (2001). *Making it in the free world: Women in transition from prison*. Albany, NY: SUNY Press.

O'Donnell, I., & Edgar, K. (1998). Routine victimization in prison. *Howard Journal of Criminal Justice, 375*, 266-279.

Parsons, T. (1937). *The structure of social action*. New York: McGraw-Hill.

Patterson, G.R. (1982). *Coercive family process*. Eugene, OR: Castalia.

Perry, D., Perry, L. & Kennedy, E. (1992). Conflict and the development of antisocial behavior. In C. Shantz & W. Hartup (Eds.). *Conflict in child and adolescent development* (pp. 301-329). Cambridge: Cambridge University Press.

Peters, L., Andrews, G., Cottler, L. B., & Chatterji, S. (1996). The Composite International Diagnostic Interview Post-Traumatic Stress Disorder module: Preliminary data. *International Journal of Methods in Psychiatric Research, 6*, 167-174.

Petersilia, J. (1994). Violent crime and violent criminals: The response of the justice system. In M. Costanzo & S. Oskamp, (Eds.), *Violence and the law (Claremont Symposium on Applied Social Psychology)*, (pp. 226-245). Thousand Oaks, CA: Sage Publications.

Peterson, L., Mullins, L. & Ridley-Johnson, R. (1985). Childhood depression: Peer reactions to depression and life stress. *Journal of Abnormal Child Psychology, 13*, 597-610.

Pew Charitable Trusts. (2007). *Public safety public spending: Forecasting America's prison population 2007–2011*. Washington, DC: Author.

Port, C. L., Engdahl, B. E., & Frazier, P. (2001). A longitudinal study of PTSD among prisoners of war. *Journal of Psychiatry, 158*, 1474-1479.

Prison Rape Elimination Act (2003) Found at http://www.nij.gov/journals/259/prison-rape.htm

Powell, T., Holt, J., & Fondacaro, K. (1997). The prevalence of mental illness among inmates in a rural state. *Law and Human Behavior, 21*(4), 427-438.

Ryan, J. P., Davis, R. K., & Yang, H. (2001). Reintegration services and the likelihood of adult imprisonment: A longitudinal study of adjudicated delinquents. *Research on Social Work Practice, 11*(3), 321-337.

Radloff, L. (1977). The CES-D: A self-report depression scale for research in the general population. *Applied Psychological Measurement, 1*(3), 385-401.

Schiff, M., El-Bassel, N., Engstrom, M., & Gilbert, L. (2002). Psychological distress and intimate physical and sexual abuse among women in methadone maintenance treatment programs. *Social Service Review, 76* (2), 302-320.

Schmid, T., & Jones, R. (1993). Ambivalent actions: Prison adaptation strategies of first-time, short-term inmates. *Journal of Contemporary Ethnography, 21*(4), 439-463.

Schwarz, E. D., & Kowalski, J. M. (1991). Posttraumatic stress disorder after a school shooting: Effects of symptom threshold selection and diagnosis by DSM-III, DSM-III-R, or proposed DSM-IV. *American Journal of Psychiatry, 148*(5), 592-597.

Seligman, M. (1975). *Helplessness: On depression, development, and death*. Oxford: W. H. Freeman.

Sentencing Project. (2010). Retrieved June 22, 2010, from: www.sentencingproject.org/pdf/Prisoners

Silberman, C. E. (1995). *Criminal violence, criminal justice* (4th Ed.). New York: Vantage Books.

Silberman, M. (1995). *A world of violence: Corrections in America*. Belmont, CA: Wadsworth.

Silverman, M., & Vega, M. (1990). Reactions of prisoners to stress as a function of personality and demographic characteristics. *International Journal of Offender Therapy and Comparative Criminology, 34*, 187-196.

Smith, C., O'Neal, H., Tobin, J., & Walshe, D. (1996). Mental disorders in an Irish prison sample. *Criminal Behavior and Mental Health, 6*, 177-183.

Solomon, Z. (2001). The impact of posttraumatic stress disorder in military situations. *Journal of Clinical Psychiatry, 62*, 11-15.

Straus, M.A. (1994). *Beating the devil out of them: Corporal punishment in American families*. New York: Lexington Books.

Sykes, G. (1958). *The society of captives: A study of a maximum security prison*. Princeton, NJ: Princeton University Press.

Sykes, G.M. & Messinger, S.L. (1960). The Inmate Social System. In R. Cloward (Ed.), *Theoretical studies in social organization of the prison*. New York: Social Science Research Council.

References

Thomas, C. (1977). Theoretical Perspectives on Prisonization: A Comparison of the Importation and Deprivation Models. *The Journal of Criminal Law and Criminology, 68*(1).

Tannenbaum, F. (1938). *Crime and the community.* Boston: Ginn.

Toch, H. (1975). *Men in crisis: Human breakdown in prison.* Chicago: Aldine.

Toch, H. (1977). *Living in prison: The ecology of survival.* New York: Free Press.

Toch, H. (1984). Quo vadis? *Canadian Journal of Criminology, 26*, 511-516.

Toch, H. (1992). *Living in prison: The ecology of survival* (2nd ed.). Washington, DC: Macmillan.

Toch, H., & Adams, K. (1989). *Coping: Maladaptation in prisons.* New Brunswick, NJ: Transaction.

Travis, J., & Lawrence, S. (2002). *Beyond the prison gates: State of parole in America.* Urban Institute. Retrieved July 3, 2003, from http://www.urban.org/UploadedPDF/310583_Beyond_prison_gates.pdf

U.S. Department of Justice. (2002). *Justice expenditures and employment, 1999.* Washington, DC: Author.

Vega, W., & Rumbaut, R. (1991). Ethnic minorities and mental health. *Annual Review of Sociology, 17*, 351-383.

Verona, E., Patrick, C. J., & Joiner, T. E. (2001). Psychopathy, antisocial personality, and suicide risk. *Journal of Abnormal Psychology, 110*, 462-470.

Western, B. (2002). The impact of incarceration on wage mobility and inequality. *American Sociological Review, 67*(4), 526-546.

Wheaton, B. (1983). Stress, personal coping resources, and psychiatric symptoms: An investigation of interactive models. *Journal of Health and Social Behavior, 24*(3), 208-229.

Wieder, D. L. (2001). Telling the convict code. In R. M. Emerson (Ed.), *Contemporary field research: Perspectives and formulations.* Prospect Heights, IL: Waveland.

Williams, S., & Halgin, R. (1995). Issues in psychotherapy supervision between the White supervisors and the Black supervisee. *The Clinical Supervisor, 13*(1), 39-61.

Williams, D.R., Yu, Y., Jackson, J.S. & Anderson, N.B. (1997). Racial differences in physical and mental health: Socioeconomic status, stress & discrimination. *Journal of Health Psychology, 2*, 335-351.

Wilson, J.Q. & Hernstein, R.J. (1985). *Crime and human nature.* New York: Simon & Schuster.

Wittchen, H., Kessler, R., Zhoa, S., & Abelson, J. (1995). Reliablility and valididty of the UM-CIDI-III-R. *Journal of Psychiatric Research, 29*, 95-110.

Wooldredge, J. D. (1994). Inmate crime and victimization in a Southwestern correctional facility. *Journal of Criminal Justice, 22*, 367-381.

Wooldredge, J. D. (1998). Inmate lifestyles and opportunities for victimization. *The Journal of Research in Crime and Delinquency, 35*(4), 480-502.

Wooldredge, J. D. (1999). Inmate experiences and psychological well-being. *Criminal Justice and Behavior, 26*, 235-250.

Wooldredge, J. D., & Carboneau, T. (1998, November). *A multilevel analysis of inmate crime*. Paper presented at the annual meeting of the American Society of Criminology, Washington, DC.

Wooldredge, J. D., Griffin, T. & Pratt, I. (2001). Considering hierarchical models for research on inmate behavior: Predicting misconduct with multilevel data. *Justice Quarterly.* 18, 203-231.

Wright, K. N. (1991). The violent and the victimized in the male prison. *Journal of Offender Rehabilitation, 16*, 1-25.

Yap, M., & Devilly, G. (2004). The role of perceived social support in crime victimization. *Clinical Psychology Review, 24*(1), 1-15.

Yehuda, R., & McFarlane, A. (1995). Conflict between current knowledge about posttraumatic stress disorder and its original conceptual basis. *American Journal of Psychiatry, 152*(12), 1705-1718.

Zamble, E., & Porporino, F. (1988). *Coping behavior and adaptation in prison inmates.* New York: Springer-Verlag.

Index

Adams, 1, 6, 7, 26, 30, 31, 32, 35, 42, 45
adjustment, 1–6, 13, 18, 19, 26, 28, 31, 35, 45, 46, 51, 56–58, 71, 87, 88, 97
age first incarcerated, 4, 6, 42, 56, 95
American Psychiatric Association, 22
Aneshensel, 64

Baker and Alfonse, 92
Belsley, 68
Berwick, 31
Breslau, 25, 31, 92
Brinded, 8, 28, 33
Bukstel, 18

cell satisfaction, 35
Center of Epidemiology Studies, 64
Chambers, 30, 94
Cohen, 4, 18, 43, 45, 90
Composite International Diagnostic Interview, 62

Conklin, 98
control variables
   age first arrested, 123
   age first prison sentence, 123
   education, 122
   race, 122
convict code, 3, 4, 6, 18, 29, 36–38, 44, 47, 48, 55, 61, 66, 68, 76–78, 80, 91, 92, 95, 96
Cooper, 31
correctional goal, 18
Cressey, 29, 89, 90

Davis, 6, 25, 31, 40, 56
Dembo, 26, 30, 94
demographic characteristics, 6
dependent variables
   convict code, 118
   inmate economy, 113
   UM-CIDI, 119
   victimization, 114
   witnessing others victimized, 116
deprivation, 9
deprivation model, 3

Diagnostic Statistical Manual, 3, 22
Ditton, 32
domain-specific experience, 54
Durkheim, 17

Edgar, 41, 42, 57, 100
education, 4, 5, 21, 25, 56, 64, 65, 99, 100, 104
exposure theory, 4, 43, 45

Federal Bureau of Prisons, 20, 53, 105
feedback loop, 17
Felson, 4, 18, 43, 45, 90
Florida Corrections Commission Annual Report, 32
frequency in the system, 4, 46–49, 65, 69, 72–75, 77, 81, 82, 95, 96
Gendreau, 7, 9, 18, 99
Goodstein, 39
Gorski, 103, 104
Gottfredson, 4, 6, 90
Greene, 6
Gujarati, 66
Guthrie, 7, 26, 45

Hemmens, 31, 42, 56
Hirschi, 6, 90

importation model, 3, 6, 89, 90
incarceration rate, 20
independent variables
  frequency in criminal justice system, 109
  negative parenting
  pre-prison criminality, 108
  streetwise, 107

inmate economy, 4, 35–37, 46, 48, 59, 60, 65, 68–72, 79, 85, 88–96
inmate victimization, 93
in-prison variables, 2, 59, 68, 69, 79, 91, 95
in-prison victimization, 4, 41, 46–48, 73–76, 79, 85, 89–92, 95
integrated model, 3
internal validity, 51, 52, 54
Irwin, 3, 29, 89, 90, 105

Jang, 29, 94
Johnson, 28

Kessler, 13, 28, 31, 62
Kuh, 68

learned helplessness, 9, 39
lifestyle theory, 4, 43, 44
Loucks, 30

MacKenzie, 39
Maitland, 41
McCorkle, 41, 99
McFarlane, 22, 31, 98
Mead, 17
medical model, 16
military veterans, 34

National Youth Survey, 57, 58
negative parenting, 47–49, 58, 65, 68, 69, 72, 74–77, 81, 83, 85, 89, 90, 93–95
nonviolent victimization, 41

orderly system of social interactions, 17
overcrowding, 21, 31, 32, 97, 99

Index

Parsons, 17
Pennsylvania System, 15
place-specific application, 43
population growth, 20
post-incarceration PTSS, 99
post-incarceration syndrome, 104
post-prison employment, 12
Post-Traumatic Stress Diagnostic Scale, 119
post-traumatic stress disorder, 22–25
post-traumatic stress symptoms, 1–13, 48, 63
Power, 30
pre-prison criminality, 4, 46, 47–49, 57, 65, 68–78, 81, 82, 88, 89, 94–96
pre-prison experience, 1, 4, 6, 13, 19, 26, 27, 30, 51, 87, 88, 89, 96, 97
pre-prison variables, 2, 4, 13, 59, 68, 69, 71, 87, 88, 93, 95, 96
pre-sentence investigation report, 54
prevalence rate, 8, 21, 34, 92
prison conditions, 8, 42
prison culture, 15, 27, 37, 59, 61
prison environment, 3–9, 13, 18, 21, 27, 28, 29, 31, 32, 35, 36, 43–45, 51, 57, 61, 71, 88, 90, 92, 95–98, 103
prison maladjustment, 31
prison management, 16
prison population, 6, 8, 19, 21, 40, 52, 92, 98, 103
prisonization/institutionalization, 17

PTSD. *See* post-traumatic stress disorder
PTSS. *See* post-traumatic stress symptoms
public health model, 98

Quakers, 15

race, 4, 5, 6, 42, 52, 56, 65, 73
Radloff, 64
recidivism, 11, 12, 99, 102, 104
redemption, 15, 16
redemptive model, 16
rehabilitation, 16, 101, 104
reintegration, 6, 11, 12, 33, 39, 98
routine activities theory, 4, 43, 46
Ryan, 6, 56

self-control, 6, 90, 93
Seligman, 39
Sentencing Commission, 103
Shortland, 39
Silverman, 27, 100
Sluder, 41
Smith, 28, 29, 94
social system, 15, 17
society, 10, 11, 15, 18, 19, 39, 102–104
solitary, 16, 19, 31, 97, 99, 103
streetwise, 4, 26, 28, 46–49, 57, 65, 68, 69, 71, 73–76, 81, 91, 94–96
subculture formation, 18
Swanson, 30
Sykes, 1, 3, 8, 9, 15, 27, 37, 41
symbolic interaction, 17

Tennessee, 42
trauma, 8, 10, 23, 24, 25, 34, 39, 98, 100
traumatic stressor, 4, 7, 9, 23

U.S. Department of Justice, 105
U.S. National Comorbidity Survey, 62
University of Michigan Composite International Diagnostic Index, 60

Vega, 27, 64, 100
Vega and Rumbaut, 64

victimization, 4, 7, 10, 30, 31, 36, 37, 40–47, 48, 60, 65, 68, 73–76, 79, 80, 85, 90, 92–99, 100
violent victimization, 41

Welsch, 68
witnessing victimization, 4, 31, 44, 61, 74–76, 78, 80, 95, 96
Wooldredge, 4, 19, 41, 42, 43, 44, 45, 46, 90, 93

Yang, 6, 56
Yehuda, 22, 98